M000284039

Revolutionary Lives

Series Editors: Sarah Irving, University of Edinburgh;
Professor Paul Le Blanc, La Roche College, Pittsburgh

Revolutionary Lives is a series of short, critical biographies of radical figures from throughout history. The books are sympathetic but not sycophantic, and the intention is to present a balanced and, where necessary, critical evaluation of the individual's place in their political field, putting their actions and achievements in context and exploring issues raised by their lives, such as the use or rejection of violence, nationalism, or gender in political activism. While individuals are the subject of the books, their personal lives are dealt with lightly except insofar as they mesh with political concerns. The focus is on the contribution these revolutionaries made to history, an examination of how far they achieved their aims in improving the lives of the oppressed and exploited, and how they can continue to be an inspiration for many today.

Also available:

Salvador Allende:
Revolutionary Democrat
Victor Figueroa Clark

Leila Khaled:
Icon of Palestinian Liberation
Sarah Irving

Jean Paul Marat:
Tribune of the French Revolution
Clifford D. Conner

Sylvia Pankhurst:
Suffragette, Socialist and Scourge of Empire
Katherine Connelly

Ellen Wilkinson:
From Red Suffragist to Government Minister
Paula Bartley

Gerrard Winstanley:
The Digger's Life and Legacy
John Gurney

www.revolutionarylives.co.uk

Hugo Chávez

Socialist for the Twenty-first Century

Mike Gonzalez

PlutoPress

www.plutobooks.com

First published 2014 by Pluto Press
345 Archway Road, London N6 5AA

www.plutobooks.com

Distributed in the United States of America exclusively by
Palgrave Macmillan, a division of St. Martin's Press LLC,
175 Fifth Avenue, New York, NY 10010

British Library Cataloguing in Publication Data
A catalogue record for this book is available from the British Library

ISBN   978 0 7453 3466 0   Hardback
ISBN   978 0 7453 3465 3   Paperback
ISBN   978 1 7837 1029 4   PDF eBook
ISBN   978 1 7837 1031 7   Kindle eBook
ISBN   978 1 7837 1030 0   EPUB eBook

Library of Congress Cataloging in Publication Data applied for

This book is printed on paper suitable for recycling and made from fully
managed and sustained forest sources. Logging, pulping and manufacturing
processes are expected to conform to the environmental standards of the
country of origin.

10   9   8   7   6   5   4   3   2   1

Typeset from disk by Stanford DTP Services, Northampton, England
Text design by Melanie Patrick
Simultaneously printed digitally by CPI Antony Rowe, Chippenham, UK and
Edwards Bros in the United States of America

For Nella
With my love my thanks
and
my admiration

Contents

List of Illustrations

Glossary

AD   Acción Democrática – A social democratic party
            founded in 1941 by Rómulo Betancourt among
            others, originally to support the Presidential
            candidacy of Rómulo Gallegos.

ALBA   The Bolivian Alternative for Latin America. An
            organisation for Latin American integration formed
            by Venezuela and Cuba in 2004.

Bandera Roja   Red Flag – formed in 1970 after splitting from MIR,
            it was a hard line Marxist-Leninist guerrilla group.
            It joined with the right wing opposition to Chávez
            and is currently part of the right-wing anti Chávez
            opposition coalition.

Cantv   Venezuelan Telephone Company.

Causa R   Radical Cause, a radical party formed in 1971 by
            Alfredo Maneiro after he split from the Communist
            Party. Influential particularly among trade
            unionists in industry in Guayana. It later divided
            over question of support for Chávez. Pro Chávez
            elements formed PPT.

Celac   Community of Latin American and Caribbean
            States, and including 33 states excluding Canada,
            the US and French and Dutch colonies. Formed in
            2011.

Coordinadora
  Democrática   Democratic Coordinating Committee.

COPEI   Christian Democratic Party, founded 1946 by Rafael
            Caldera.

CTV   Venezuelan Trade Union Congress, led by Carlos
            Ortega who played a leading role in the coup against
            Chávez.

FALN   Armed Forces of National Liberation – Guerrilla
            organisation formed in 1962. After his split from

ix

	the Communist Party Douglas Bravo became its acknowledged leader.
Fedecámaras	Federation of Chambers of Commerce (National Employers Federation).
FBT	Bolivarian Labour Front, formed to replace the CTV under Chávez, led by Marcela Maspero and Franklin Rondon.
MAS	Movement Toward Socialism – a split from the Communist Party led by ex-guerrilla Teodoro Petkoff, later to split over its attitude to Chávez.
MBR-200	Bolivarian Revolutionary Movement – clandestine group within the army formed by Chávez and three others.
Mercosur	Common Market for Latin America.
MIR	Movement of the Revolutionary Left – split from AD in 1960 and merged with MAS in 1988, after several splits of its own.
MUD	Democratic Unity Roundtable, political alliance formed in 2008 to bring together opposition to Chávez.
MVR	Movement of the Fifth Republic – Political organisation formed by Chávez and allies for the 1998 elections.
OPEC (OPEP in Spanish)	Organisation of Petroleum Exporting Countries formed in 1960.
PCV	Venezuelan Communist Party – founded in 1931, the party has suffered a number of splits. In 1998 it joined the Polo Patriótico to support Chávez in the presidential election. It became estranged from him after the formation of PSUV.
Pdvsa	Venezuelan National Oil Corporation.
Polo Patriótico	Patriotic Pole – Electoral coalition formed to support Chávez's candidacy in 1998.
PPT	Patria Para Todos – A nation for all. Split from Causa R in 1998 over support for Chávez's

	presidential bid. Included Alí Rodríguez Araque, Aristóbulo Istúriz and others.
PRV	Party of the Venezuelan Revolution – formed by Douglas Bravo after his expulsion from the Venezuelan Communist Party in 1966.
PSUV	United Socialist Party of Venezuela – formed by Chávez after his re-election in December 2006.
RCTV	Radio Caracas TV – television and radio broadcaster.
Unasur	Latin American intergovernmental union formed in 2008 merging Mercosur and the Andean Commercial Union (CAN). Its headquarters are in Ecuador.
UNT	National Labour Union – formed originally in 2003 by a group of left organisations. Its first Congress, in April 2007, was disrupted and UNT subsequently split.
URD	Radical Democratic Union – a small radical party it was in alliance with AD after the overthrow of Pérez Jiménez in 1958. It split from AD in 1960 over its attitude to Cuba. Its leader Fabricio Ojeda later joined the guerrillas.

Timeline

1783   Birth of Simón Bolívar in Caracas.

1786   After his mother's death, Bolívar is entrusted to the care of his black maid, La Negra Hipólita, and various tutors, the most important and influential of whom was Simón Rodríguez, alias 'Robinson'.

1807   Bolívar returns to Venezuela from Europe.

1811   Venezuelan Independence Act passed.

1812   (*March*) Caracas earthquake. (*June*) Battle of Carabobo between independence fighters, led by Bolívar, and Royalist forces. Bolívar is victorious.

1813   Bolívar launches his 'Admirable Campaign'.

1821   State of Gran Colombia created with Bolívar as president.

1824   Battle of Ayacucho at which General Sucre inflicts a definitive defeat on the Spanish armies.

1830   (*April*) Bolívar resigns as president of Gran Colombia. (*December*) Death of Bolívar from tuberculosis in Santa Marta, Colombia.

1912   First Venezuelan oil well drilled near Maracaibo.

1908–35 Dictatorship of Juan Vicente Gómez.

1948   Brief (ten months) presidency of Rómulo Gallegos.

1952   Marcos Pérez Jiménez takes power in a military coup.

1954   Hugo Chávez Frías born in Sabaneta, Barinas province, Venezuela.

1958   (*January*) Marcos Pérez Jiménez overthrown by a mass insurrection. (*December*) Rómulo Betancourt of Acción Democrática elected to the presidency.

1959   Cuban Revolution led by Fidel Castro triumphs.

1971   Chávez enters Military Academy.

1973   (*September*) Salvador Allende, head of Chile's Popular Unity government, is overthrown in a military coup led by Augusto Pinochet. Allende is killed. (*October*) Oil price rise as a result of the Arab–Israeli War.

1974	150th anniversary of the battle of Ayacucho. Chávez visits Peru.
1975	Chávez graduates from the Military Academy.
1976	Military dictatorship established in Argentina.
1979	(*July*) Nicaraguan revolution led by the Sandinistas ends the Somoza dictatorship.
1983	Military dictatorship in Argentina falls in the wake of the Falklands/Malvinas conflict.
1989	Carlos Andrés Pérez elected to the Presidency. Caracazo (a wave of protests) begins after the announcement of austerity measures.
1992	(*February*) Coup led by Hugo Chávez. It fails and he is arrested. (*November*) Attempted coup led by Admiral Grueber and Air Force General Visconti.
1994	Chávez released from prison.
1996	Carlos Andrés Pérez imprisoned after being convicted on fraud charges.
1998	(*December*) Hugo Chávez Frias elected to the Presidency of Venezuela.
1999	(*February*) Chávez inaugurated as President. (*March*) Vote on referendum for a new Constitution. (*May*) Constituent Assembly elected to draw up a new Constitution. (*November*) Referendum approves the new Bolivarian Constitution. Devastating mudslides engulf the state of Vargas.
2000	(*May*) Chávez elected to the Presidency under the new Constitution. Chávez visits Iraq.
2001	(*November*) Chávez introduces 49 new pieces of legislation under the Enabling Law.
2002	(*February*) Chávez appoints new board of directors to state oil company Pdvsa. (*11 April*) Chávez arrested after a coup. New government declared. (*14 April*) Chávez resumes the Presidency. (*December*) Bosses strike initiated.
2003	(*March*) Bosses strike ends. (*December*) Recall referendum petition delivered with 3.4 million signatures.
2004	(*August*) Recall referendum confirms Chávez as President for the remaining part of his six-year term.

2005   (*December*) Parties loyal to Chávez make gains in National
       Assembly elections which are boycotted by the opposition
       leaving an Assembly consisting entirely of Chávez
       supporters.

2006   (*December*) Chávez elected to the Presidency with
       increased majority. Formation of PSUV announced.

2007   (*January*) Nationalisation of telecommunications and
       oil companies. (*May*) RCTV closed down. (*December*)
       Chávez loses a referendum vote for the first time, when his
       proposals for new constitutional clauses are rejected by a
       narrow majority.

2008   (*March*) Colombian military cross the border into Ecuador
       to attack a Farc camp. Farc leader Raul Reyes killed in the
       raid. (*July*) Release of Ingrid Betancourt, held by the Farc.
       Uribe, president of Colombia, visits Venezuela for talks
       with Chávez. (*November*) Regional elections produce gains
       for the opposition. Government loses five governorships
       and the mayoralty of Caracas. Venezuela and Russia sign
       agreement for oil and gas cooperation.

2009   (*February*) Voters in a referendum approve a clause
       allowing public officials, including the President, to serve
       multiple terms. (*August*) Rising tensions with Colombia as
       Bogotá accuses Chávez of supporting the Farc guerrillas.

2010   (*January*) Devaluation of the Bolívar (the Venezuelan
       currency). (*September*) Elections to the National assembly.
       Opposition makes gains. PSUV still has the majority, but it
       is reduced. (*October*) Chávez visits Iran.

2011   (*June*) Chávez embarks on a year-long course of treatment
       for cancer in Cuba. (*November*) Government introduces
       price controls to address 27 per cent inflation rate.

2012   (*June*) Chávez announced that he had completed his
       course of treatment for cancer and was ready to stand
       in the presidential election. (*July*) Globovisión, an
       anti-Chávez television station, pays a $2.1 million fine for
       its coverage of a prison riot; (*December*) Chávez, though
       absent, is re-elected to the Presidency.

2013   (*January*) Inauguration of Chávez as President. He is too ill to take the oath. Thousands of people fill streets and squares to take the oath on his behalf. (*March*) Death of Hugo Chávez from cancer. (*April*) Nicolás Maduro elected President of Venezuela.

(A young boy converses with Simon Bolívar)

Boy: Oh if you could see the destiny
Of the peoples you liberated with your sword
They have more liberty now
To die of hunger
Crushed by the northern boot
That you warned us about … .
And looking straight at the boy
Bolívar said: take my spurs
Go from town to town
Wake the people up
Tell them to raise their heads
To make history again.

Ali Primera, 'Bolívar'

Introduction:
A Man for Difficult Times[1]

Hugo Chávez was nothing if not controversial. In Venezuela, his presidency provoked deep divisions, or rather exposed divisions that already existed.

When he died, on 5 March 2013, a majority of Venezuelans mourned his passing with genuine grief; but there were harsh reactions to the news of his illness from that section of the population who had opposed him throughout his presidency. Outside the country, opinions were equally polarised. The Spanish press was consistently critical of him, and in the United States successive administrations alleged that he was part of the 'Axis of Evil'. But there was an equally large, if not larger, number of people for whom his scorn for protocol, his eloquent attacks on neo-liberalism, his solidarity with the struggles of the oppressed, earned him their admiration and support.

Venezuela had not figured large in the consciousness of the world in previous years. It was an important oil producer and a member of OPEC – people did know that – and it produced a number of winning entrants to the Miss World contests, star baseball players and boxing champions. But it always surprised me how many people would ask where it was, and what language was spoken there. In the second decade of the twenty-first century, however, the more likely response in most parts of the world to the mention of Venezuela's name has been 'Hugo Chávez', often accompanied by a smile. His famous appearance at the United Nations speaker's podium immediately after George W. Bush – or 'Mr Danger' as he used to call him – had spoken, when he commented that you could still smell the sulphur, endeared him to those many millions who had marched across the world on 23 February 2003 in protest at the Iraq War.

Chávez's first interventions in national politics, as this biography traces, began while he was a military officer organising small conspiratorial cells of dissidents.

Many of them, like him, came from poor backgrounds and still felt a connection and an allegiance to their class. Yet despite this early experience, Hugo Chávez became a spokesperson for a very different kind of politics, neither a guerrilla strategy nor clandestine conspiracies, but a vision of participatory democracy. The trigger for this new way of thinking about how societies change was an event that marked a critical conjuncture in Venezuela's modern history – the insurrectionary rising of Venezuela's marginalised populations called the *Caracazo*, on 27 February 1989. This explosion of rage and frustration was a reaction to the imposition of a neo-liberal package of emergency economic measures called euphemistically 'structural adjustment'. Translated, this meant massive cuts in social spending, the privatisation of industry and services in public ownership, and a consequent collapse of the standard of living of most Venezuelans. These austerity measures became painfully familiar throughout Latin America in the decade that followed.

At the same time, the *Caracazo* was an early form of a new kind of struggle – mass social movements mounting a sustained and determined resistance structured around innovative organisational methods. Sometimes these were expressed in the language of community, sometimes by historical references long buried in popular culture, sometimes in the symbolic universe of grassroots religion. Analysts in the West referred to these groupings collectively as 'civil society'; yet they were very different from the largely middle-class pressure groups or the NGOs that in the 1990s came to take the place of absent representative institutions in Latin America and elsewhere. The collapse of Stalinism had discredited and disoriented the socialist tradition; and privatisation brought widespread industrial closures and a crisis on the land as global capital overwhelmed small scale agricultural production. The marginalisation of whole communities, the explosive growth of the precarious sector of the economy and the dispossession of indigenous populations generated responses that were framed in unfamiliar ways. The NGOs, most of which originated in Europe or America, operated in a familiar territory of political negotiation; the new social movements grew up on a different terrain – the poor barrios, the isolated indigenous communities, the peasant communities fighting for their very survival, often against ruthless landowners. And they would respond to their alienation in different ways – with explosions of rage, or forms of local self-help. They produced their own leaders and their own imaginary. But they tended, at least at first, to remain local and uncoordinated.

Throughout the 1990s, neo-liberalism continued its destructive march across the globe. But it always met resistance, exemplified by the Zapatista rising in southern Mexico in January 1994. That movement was quickly isolated physically in the state of Chiapas, where the Zapatista communities were surrounded by over 60,000 soldiers. But its political message reached most corners of the world, thanks to the newly developed worldwide web, which was intended for use by the powerful, not the powerless. That message argued for a democratic and egalitarian society, an alternative to the merciless neo-liberal order and its spurious democracies. Like the social movements, the Zapatistas organised horizontally and rejected the hierarchical forms of existing parties. Its most prominent spokesman called himself *Sub*comandante Marcos – an explicit acknowledgment that the leadership was collective and that he was subject to it. By the end of the decade resistance to globalisation had spread across the planet – in the anti-capitalist movements of Europe and the US, in the rejection of the New American Century proposed by Bush and his allies, in the burgeoning movements of solidarity with Palestine, and in Latin America in a rising tide of refusal to accept any longer the demands of the neo-liberal strategies that had wreaked such havoc there for over a decade.

In Bolivia, the Cochabamba water war in 2000 united every section of the city's population in its rejection of the government's decision to privatise water. It was emblematic. This was a battle about the unequal distribution of wealth, the exploitation of the region's resources for the benefit of global capital, the destruction of the environment, and the absence of democratic control. And the struggle was organised in local assemblies where decisions were taken in open debate. In Ecuador in that same year, the indigenous organisations united with the trade unions in a successful struggle against 'dollarization', in other words the absorption of Ecuador's economy into the global market.

Figure 1.1   Hugo Chávez (© Luis Noguera)

Hugo Chávez's victory in the Venezuelan presidential election in December 1998, coincided with these events. His inaugural address two months later was a sign of things to come, and testimony to how different he was from all previous occupants of the post. He denounced the national constitution and proposed the immediate election of a Constituent Assembly to draw up a new constitution that acknowledged the rights of all Venezuelans and undertook to use the nation's resources for the benefit of the majority rather than the profit of a few. Although he came from a military background, his language and manner expressed clearly how closely he identified with both the vision and the spirit of the emerging anti-globalisation movement (it is significant that in Spanish the movement is called *altermundista*, a movement for another world).

The new constitution, passed by an overwhelming majority in a referendum, renamed Venezuela as a Bolivarian Republic. While most south Americans, and particularly Venezuelans, were familiar with Bolívar's image and some elements of his story, it was not immediately clear what Chávez meant by the term. What was generally understood was that the process that he had inaugurated was Latin American in its ideas and inspiration, and took from Bolívar two key concepts – the struggle for national independence, or sovereignty, and the inescapable necessity of regional integration and unity. In Chávez's interpretation of Bolívar, national self-determination was still to be achieved; imperialism's hold had not yet been broken, but empire could be successfully resisted and a new society, just and egalitarian, be created.

In Venezuela this had a particular resonance. Since the discovery of oil, and its appropriation by largely US-based oil companies, Venezuela had become one of the world's most important oil-producing states. The income from the 'black gold' was enormous. The older forms of agricultural production collapsed, and oil dominated the economy. Yet that immense wealth was not equally distributed. Two ferociously repressive military regimes oversaw the early period of oil production. The Gómez dictatorship was succeeded after a brief interregnum by the military rule of Marcos Pérez Jiménez. His overthrow by a mass movement in 1958 led to the establishment of a bourgeois democracy, hailed from then on as a model for Latin America. Yet the reality of that exemplary democracy was very different from the claims made for it. Two populist parties, Acción Democrática and the Christian Democrat COPEI, signed an agreement to share power and distribute the lucrative government posts between them. The beneficiaries of their patronage grew rich on the fraction of oil profits that remained in Venezuela. But the majority of the society found themselves living in the mushrooming shanty towns in and around the major cities, fruitlessly anticipating that they too would gain from the endlessly gushing black liquid.

When protests began and elements of the left mounted a struggle against that corrupt elite, the democracy revealed its true face, torturing and killing opponents and introducing the world for the first time to the concept of 'the disappeared'.

It was this situation, persisting into the 1990s, that Hugo Chávez promised to reverse. And because he did not come from the privileged and corrupt elite who mimicked the American way of life and freely spent the oil profits, he won the support of the poor and the marginalised. His promise of a new participatory democracy echoed the experience of a decade of popular resistance. And the arguments about national sovereignty made considerable sense when they began with the declaration that the fruits of the subsoil, the oil and the gas, should benefit all Venezuelans, and not the imperialist power to the north which had grown fat at their expense. The message resonated through the mass movements in Cochabamba, Quito, Buenos Aires as well as Caracas, where the masses were beginning to take the streets and transform them into democratic spaces.

Chávez was initially convinced that in a parliamentary democracy like Venezuela these changes could take place. But while the political institutions were now ostensibly Chavista, the state itself, the economy, the mass media, the education sector were still dominated by the old ruling order. And they were unwilling to allow a man from the wrong side of the tracks, with the wrong skin colour and the wrong accent to wrest power from the bourgeoisie. They fought back, in relentless and violent ways, culminating in an attempted coup and later in an attack on the economy itself in 2002. The response from Venezuela's masses, who mobilised to defend the new order, saved Chávez and marked the beginning of a Bolivarian revolution – the entry of the mass movement on to the stage of history as actors, as its subjects. But the enemies of that revolution continued their attack, combining economic sabotage with a sustained media campaign.

When he came to power, Chávez encountered a political system that was broken, a left that was fragmented and disoriented and mass movements that were combative and determined but disorganised and uncoordinated among themselves. The coup of 2002 and the attempt to destroy the economy by the right-wing parties and the economic elite later that year both failed because the *pueblo*, the people, had fought back and defended Chávez's project. The revolution, as a transfer of power from one class to another, really began there rather than with the election victory of 1998. But in the absence of any form of political organisation capable of coordinating and providing political direction to those movements, leadership devolved back upon Chávez. The state remained under the domination of the old functionaries who devised a thousand ways to sabotage and undermine the radical possibilities that Chávez represented.

The alternative was to mobilise the forces of the excluded, the social base of Chavismo, to challenge that state and wrest control from it. Instead, Chávez chose to conduct the process himself, in the conviction that he shared with Simón Bolívar, his hero and mentor, that the masses would first have to be prepared for power. He was not, as even the relentlessly hostile Rory Carroll[2] recognises, an autocrat or an authoritarian. He was not corrupt, as many of his immediate collaborators were or became. But by his second presidential term, beginning in 2006, he had clearly come to see himself as indispensable to the process of change. And that was the paradox of Chávez. Because this was the same man who had placed on the political agenda of the whole of the left the prospect of a new and different world, just and egalitarian, and governed by an authentic democracy and a profound sense of international solidarity, a world in which the people governed themselves.

By 2006, faced with the complex realities of rebuilding an economy in the context of a capitalist world market, Chávez had sought out allies who did not share his commitment to the twenty-first socialism whose imminence he had announced at the World Social Forum in January 2005. Russia and China were commercial partners and nothing more; their priorities were those of any capitalist economy and their relationships with other countries built on the realisation of profit. Yet Chávez began to present them as an alternative to the imperialism of the United States, as if these new partners were not driven by the same motivations as the US-based multinationals. The increasingly close relations with Iran and Libya, for example, certainly bore no relation to the global spread of a new participatory democracy, but to the mutual interest of state capitals creating negotiating blocks in a global economy. In Latin America, the Bolivarian Alternative, ALBA, was closer to the collaborative alliance envisaged by Bolívar, and there were real social advances in member countries as a result. But it was not socialism, either in terms of collective ownership or in terms of participation.

And in the absence of an organised people to which he was subject and accountable beyond regular elections, Chávez in his later years was to become increasingly dependent on a new bureaucracy which began to take on the characteristics – corruption, inefficiency, favouritism – of the old. And the real social advances that millions of Venezuelans had enjoyed as a result of Chávez's rise to power now began to fracture and fail. There is a sense, as he neared death, that Chávez was becoming aware of the problem, or at least that he was beginning to acknowledge it. In the end he nominated Nicolas Maduro to be his successor and he was duly elected in March 2013. As yet it is not clear in what direction Maduro is taking Venezuela, or whether he will be able to realise the dream of a new democracy in which the majority and their interests control the future.

What has Chávez left behind? Against the background of the end of Stalinism and the political crisis that ensued, great hopes were placed in Chávez as symbolising a new political direction. And as so often happens, that hope was so great that it veiled the contradictions at the heart of the Chávez project which would inhibit its ability to reach its stated objective – a socialism for the twenty-first century that was not Stalinist, that was genuinely democratic, that cared for the environment, that fought oppression, that built international solidarity and that rejected capitalist values. Many of Chávez's words will inspire the resistance and the struggle for socialism in the future; but the political practices that he oversaw were often in conflict with their claims, and that too will serve the next generation of revolutionaries, as a lesson and a warning.

1

The Plainsman

Local Heroes

In his many long conversations with the Venezuelan people – on radio, television, in his public speeches and his writings – Hugo Chávez would always explain his political decisions by reference to some aspect of his own story. It was a constant reminder to his largely poor and working-class supporters of their shared history. In this highly political narrative, its central figure was a man who came from outside the prevailing political system and brought with him to the presidential palace a memory his adoring audience would recognise and approve. The facts are often not in question – but their significance, their resonance in the subsequent biography of Hugo Rafael Chávez Frías, coloured and dramatised those facts, until his life story became an alternative history of Venezuela.

He was born near Sabaneta de Barinas in Venezuela's llanos region, the wide grasslands whose inhabitants are renowned for their horsemanship, their resistance to the authority of a distant Caracas, and their general reserve – at least until trust is established, at which stage they become voluble and generous. Hugo's father was a rural schoolteacher whose pitiful salary did not stretch to maintaining his and his wife Elena's six children. The Chávez household was poor, though not the 'mud hut' one biographer[1] has attributed to him. And Hugo's father was an active member of Acción Democrática, one of Venezuela's two dominant political parties. At the age of four, Hugo and his older brother Adán were sent to Sabaneta itself into the care of his grandmother, Rosa Inés. The town had four streets and a thousand or so inhabitants. Even allowing for the exaggerations that nostalgia brings, Rosa Inés was an enduring influence on both brothers. It is often suggested that the young Hugo grew increasingly distant from his mother; what is certainly true is that his grandmother became a constant reference point and the object of his enduring affection. She made sweets for a living, which Hugo sold in the street after school. At home she spoke frequently about the history of the area, and recalled with obvious pride the activities of Hugo's great grandfather Maisanta, described by some as a local bandit and by others as a courageous local freedom fighter who resisted the influence of the *caudillos*[2] of Caracas. Rosa Inés clearly saw him as heroic, and that was the image that she transmitted to young Hugo. And she was interested in her country's history more generally, although her formal education was minimal. That may have been one component in Hugo's lifelong fascination with the key historical figures in Venezuela's past, and his identification with them.

Rosa Inés was as poor as his parents, but Hugo always insisted that his childhood was happy and protected. His mother recalls that his two enthusiasms were art and baseball. A pitcher, he modelled himself on his namesake, Isaías Chávez, who played in the US leagues and was known as The Whip (*El Látigo*). Since baseball is Venezuela's national sport, and the US leagues were the golden road to fame and fortune for impecunious young ball players, Chávez's ambitions were neither unusual nor unpredictable.

Hugo never did get his trial for the US Majors, but his enthusiasm for baseball was responsible for his next, fateful step. While there was no scope for his sporting ambition in Sabaneta, the military academy in Caracas had its own team, although Chávez was a lifelong supporter of their rivals, the Navegantes de Magallanes, from Valencia. The legend is that Hugo signed up for the military at the age of 17 fundamentally because he thought he would be able to play baseball there. That might feed the impression of a reluctant politician thrust into public life by an overwhelming sense of duty, but the image of a retiring Hugo Chávez eschewing the limelight barely fits with the life he lived. In any event, the more compelling reason for taking up a place at the Academy (which he finally achieved by the skin of his teeth, with his baseball skills finally tipping the balance after he failed a chemistry test) was the educational opportunity it provided for young men of slender means and of provincial background. In this the Venezuelan military was unlike other military establishments in

Figure 2.1 Chávez entering military academy
(© Luis Noguera)

Latin America.[3] Its career structure was meritocratic, and it was not unusual for people of Chávez's background to rise rapidly through the officer class. Many of the commanding officers on whom Chávez would later rely came from a similar background to his own. And his arrival at the Academy, in August 1971, coincided with the implementation of a new curriculum, the Plan Andrés Bello, which led to a university degree rather than a purely military qualification. Political science was studied side by side with military history and the history of Venezuela; Chávez would later specialise in engineering and communication studies. His reading lists included Marx and Mao as well as Clausewitz.

While they were still living with Rosa Inés it was Hugo's brother Adán rather than him who expressed an early interest in politics. His best friends at home were the three sons of a local historian, José Esteban Ruiz Guevara, a communist; he will have heard constant political discussion in their house, where he spent a great deal of time, but the reality is that there is no evidence of a precocious social concern in the young Hugo. Baseball, the cinema and girls seemed his main interests. This suggests that the awakening of his political consciousness began in the Academy, although some biographers claim that he arrived as a cadet carrying Che Guevara's Bolivian Diary.[4] Chávez himself denied it. But what is important are the influences and experiences that shaped his rapidly growing awareness.

Chávez entered the Academy in 1971 and graduated three years later, at the age of 21. In keeping with the learning environment he found himself in, with its military emphasis, he and his generation were especially aware of important events elsewhere on the continent – in Panama, in Chile and in Peru in particular – in which the military played a key role, with very different results, as we shall see below.

On his visits home, grandma Rosa Inés would light a votive candle in the hope that young Hugo would give up the army; she had always disapproved of his decision to enter the Academy. But in fact it was his dream of a career on the baseball diamond that was fading, and in one letter to her he expressed his pride in the uniform he wore and the group he was part of. Late in 1971 he visited the grave in Caracas of his childhood idol, Isaías Chávez (who had died in a plane crash), to close that chapter with an apology to his dead hero. And while he still expressed little explicit interest in politics, he was becoming increasingly absorbed in the history of his country, which he read as an extraordinary epic of struggle led by outstanding individuals like Simón Bolívar, Simón Rodríguez (who called himself 'Robinson') and Ezequiel Zamora with whom he shared the dream of 'Free men in a free land and a horror of the oligarchy', Zamora's famous war cry. He read Bolívar avidly and developed at an early age that impressive ability to quote huge chunks from memory at the drop of a hat – which he would continue to do throughout the rest of his life.

Among his colleagues at the Academy were the two sons of General Omar Torrijos, who had taken power in Panama in 1968 with a programme of social reform and anti-imperialism. Torrijos clearly identified with the Cuban revolution, though his enemy was a corrupt ruling class long protected by the colossus of the north – indeed Panama had been created as a separate country in 1903 when it declared its independence – with active support from Washington – from a Colombia then ruled by a nationalist government. Torrijos represented a body of thought which argued that the military could play a progressive role in carrying forward processes of social reform. It was an idea that had gained currency among North American political scientists in particular in the wake of the Cuban Revolution, and which had informed Kennedy's Alliance for Progress project; its aim was to support reforms carried out under controlled and guided conditions, as a counter to the Cuban example. This new ideology fitted well with the prevailing philosophy within the Venezuelan military as it had been articulated by Rafael Caldera, president of the country at that time. Against a background of organisations dedicated to armed struggle modelled on Che Guevara's narrative of the Cuban experience, this appeared to offer an alternative to both military repression (Argentina and Guatemala were current examples) and social revolution. Torrijos was a radical nationalist in a Panama dominated more directly than any other country in Latin America. Although he was personally close to Fidel Castro, he made no claim to be a socialist.

Hugo's visit as part of a delegation to Peru in 1974 to attend the ceremonies to commemorate the Battle of Ayacucho in 1824, the last great battle of the war of independence, however, seemed to have a more direct and powerful influence on him. Juan Velasco Alvarado, the then military president of Peru, had inaugurated – also in 1968 – what he called 'the Peruvian national revolution', the title of his book, of which he gave a copy to each member of the delegation. Velasco had set out to modernise Peru, to challenge its antiquated forms of landholding and to establish democratic procedures. The fundamental problem, however, which Chávez did not acknowledge then or later, was that his Cabinet consisted entirely of military personnel and that the process of change he proposed was to be conducted entirely from above. The mass organisation he created, Sinamos, to carry through land and social reform to benefit Peru's indigenous population did not include representatives of those communities. Instead it created new layers of bureaucracy, who were the direct beneficiaries of the state programmes, while fulfilling none of the objectives of integration and representation that his 'national revolution' promised.[5] When the Velasco government was overthrown less than a year later by an internal right-wing coup, there was no resistance from a disillusioned mass movement. Nevertheless, a Chávez slightly starstruck after his meeting with Velasco, carried his book with him for several years, he claims, as 'bedtime reading'.

The third major political event of Chávez's Academy years still resonates around the world over 40 years later. On 11 September 1973, the elected Popular Unity government of Chile led by Salvador Allende was overthrown by a military coup headed by Augusto Pinochet. At the time, Pinochet was little known outside the country, as also, unfortunately, was his history of involvement in repression within Chile. Since then, of course, that name has become synonymous with violence, savage cruelty, and the forced subordination of the mass of the people to the exigencies of capital. Even at the time, however, the Chilean events exemplified the role the army had played until then in most Latin American countries, and would continue to play in many, as an instrument of coercion and control in defence of minority vested interests. 'Torrijos made me a follower of Torrijos, Velasco made me a Velasquista, and Pinochet made me an anti-Pinochetista', Chávez said.[6]

The Academy had transformed Hugo Chávez in many ways, but he remained the charming and loquacious young man who had gone there dreaming of the Yankee Stadium. He enthusiastically participated in cultural events at the Academy, and an early photograph shows him as master of ceremonies at a beauty contest. Yet he now saw himself as a soldier and a man with a social and political vocation expressed through historical and military references, as his devotion to Bolívar grew and his project of national liberation evolved.

Chávez graduated from the Academy in July 1975, seventh in his year. He received his diploma from the hands of Carlos Andrés Pérez, the president who came to symbolise for Chávez the Venezuela he was dedicated to transforming. Their future meetings would be very different! Chávez still had no particular political affiliation but his reading of Bolívar and the other heroes of the Independence struggle was triggering changes in his thinking. The Academy's programme included, as was to be expected, counter-guerrilla training and its accompanying ideology, but Chile had been a stark reminder of the implications of that training. He told Bart Jones that the coup against Allende had been a brutal shock, and that he and others became convinced that the coup might never have happened had the people been armed and the military moved to the side of the people. In the debates across the international left that followed the coup, this was a central question; how would the soldiers react in the face of a revolution, and how critical was it that the mass movement should have its own weapons to confront the forces of the state.[7] It was one of the questions that absorbed an international left that had been shaken to the core by Chilean events, and one that would occupy a central place in his own thinking about how social change can come about.

Yet Chávez was still only 21 years old, and his political contacts were indirect. His good friends the Ruiz Guevara boys had joined Causa R, a political organisation that would have a significant role during the 1980s. Its founder, Alfredo Maneiro, was a communist who had fought with the guerrillas before founding a new party committed to working within the organisations of the working class in a clear Marxist framework. Everyone who came into contact with Maneiro describes him as charismatic and powerful, and he played an important part in Chávez's development at a later stage. But the newly promoted second lieutenant was still absorbed by Bolívar and his independence struggle. His instinctive 'horror at the oligarchy' now merged with a growing nationalism and a class instinct that was deeply affected by the gulf between Venezuela's wealthy elites and the majority who lived in a visible poverty.

Venezuela Before Chávez

The first commercial oil wells in Venezuela were drilled in 1912. By the 1920s Venezuela had become the largest oil producer in the world.

Under the military dictatorship of Juan Vicente Gómez (1908–35) the country was transformed from an agricultural economy based on cocoa and coffee, and dominated by the landed oligarchy, into a modern economy whose aspirations were captured in the public buildings and monumental projects that reproduced the cities of Europe. Gómez was the archetypal military dictator, represented in the Spanish writer Vicente Blasco Ibanez's famous novel *Tirano Banderas*. He was absolutely authoritarian, remorseless with his enemies, with grandiose aspirations expressed most dramatically in his unfinished project to create a new city within a mountain. The funding for these plans came from an oil industry dominated and controlled by foreign – mainly US-based – oil corporations. Gomez distributed over 30 million hectares of land in oil concessions, land which was then permanently lost to agriculture. The profits of this production were exported to the headquarters of the corporations, but the minimal royalties that remained in Venezuela were enough to sustain the living standards of a small urban and rural elite. In a real sense, by the late 1930s Venezuela's future was sealed – as an oil economy, dependent on its exports to acquire the consumer goods and industrial products it did not itself produce. During the 1940s more progressive nationalist governments attempted to raise the level of taxes imposed on the corporations. More radical voices, such as Pérez Alfonso, the founder of OPEC, argued for a 50–50 split of oil profits. The interregnum between 1945 and 1948 was dominated by Acción Democrática (AD), a populist mass party which went on to dominate Venezuelan politics for the next 50 years. AD led a coalition with the Communist Party (hence the designation *adeco* for its members). It reflected the post-war settlement that reproduced briefly the wartime alliances which survived until the advent of the Cold War made such alliances impossible. The original 1945 AD government was brought to power in a military coup in which Marcos Pérez Jiménez, a general of lower-middle-class provincial background, figured prominently. In 1947 the introduction of universal suffrage brought the prominent writer Rómulo Gallegos to the presidency, but he barely lasted ten months in power before he was driven out by another Pérez Jiménez-led coup. It was clear that foreign oil interests were much relieved at the removal of a democratic government intent on a more just and equitable distribution of oil profits.

Pérez Jiménez went on to rule effectively from 1948, though his formal presidency began in 1952 and lasted for six years. In that time he built a new Venezuela that announced to the world its arrival as an oil wealthy nation. It was Pérez Jiménez who commissioned the imaginative architectural projects which made Caracas the symbol of artistic Modernism. The sweeping avenues that crossed the city in the U-shaped valley overseen by the Avila mountain at the centre of the range that sheltered the city from the sea were a dramatic expression of new wealth; these wide avenues were built for the huge American cars that would speed across and above the city on the virtually free gasoline that fed them. The adventurous constructions of Carlos Raúl Villanueva, in particular the Central University, were visions of a new world that echoed Niemeyer's spectacular buildings in Brazil. And Venezuela's artists, Cruz Diez and Soto, reflected the same experimental and visionary aspirations in their kinetic work. These were the symbolic representations of the modernity that Pérez Jiménez promised, financed and guaranteed by the country's expanding oil wealth. As with every oil boom, one section of the population benefitted significantly – those who administered the new plans through the agency of the state and those who ran the oil industry on behalf of the multinational companies – known at the time as the Seven Sisters – who controlled its supply and distribution across the planet. As the oil price rose – though Venezuela garnered only a fraction of the profits generated – Pérez Jiménez paid for the new extravagant manifestations of the new wealth. But its unequal distribution left the majority of Venezuela's population – the people living in the growing slum areas around Caracas and other major cities – in poverty. The response of the Pérez Jiménez government to any protest or demonstration, however, was summary and brutal. The order that prevailed on the streets, on which people still comment nostalgically today, was the other face of a fearsome repressive apparatus.

Towards the end of 1957, Pérez Jiménez withdrew the concessions to the major multinationals and gave them instead to other, smaller, independent producers. Perhaps he imagined that this would put

Venezuela in a better position to bargain for an increased royalty. Whatever the reasons, the Sisters were angered by his insolence. And the poor in their hillside slums were reaching a point of rage. That popular anger exploded on 23 January 1958 – an iconic date in Venezuela's political history.

It is unlikely that the four-year-old Hugo Chávez, living at a considerable distance from Caracas or Maracay, the epicentres of the popular uprising, will have felt any resonance from those events at the time. Yet its echoes and consequences, politically and socially, certainly shaped Chávez's own political history. The January rising against Pérez Jiménez had been preceded by the resistance of the employers organisation Fedecámaras to the new arrangements for oil production. More crucially, the universities had risen up towards the end of 1957 in protest against repression and in defence of University autonomy. A two-month long university strike set the tone for January, and drew in the two crucial forces which successfully brought down the Pérez regime. On 1 January 1958, two military units led by Hugo Trejo and Martin Parada declared themselves in rebellion against the government. In the days that followed street fighting broke out in the barrios, the slum districts of Caracas and elsewhere.

Throughout 1957 resistance to the Pérez Jiménez regime mounted, at street level, in the universities, and in workplaces. At the same time a clandestine political alliance that included Acción Democrática and the Venezuelan Communist Party among others had formed the Junta Patriótica (the Patriotic Junta), led by the highly respected Fabricio Ojeda, in preparation for his overthrow.[8] Both the main parties were proscribed under the dictatorship, despite the fact that Pérez Jiménez had worked closely with AD just a decade earlier. The overthrow of the dictatorship, the 'fourth social uprising' in Venezuela's history, was precipitated by what Bravo calls 'social violence' as opposed to a guerrilla war or a political revolution. Every section of the population that had been denied a voice under the dictatorship played its role, creating 'democratic spaces' in which there began to emerge embryonic forms of radical grassroots organisation. Many of the participants certainly owed allegiance to AD; but it was clear that while AD supported the overthrow of the regime, their strategy was to take power in the existing state. And while there were elements on the left of the party that envisaged the possibility of a social revolution built out of the new organs of struggle that had emerged during the rising, the leadership of AD certainly did not share their view.

From exile Rómulo Betancourt, the leader of AD, was quick to see the dangers of a more far-reaching social upheaval. As soon as the uprising happened, on 23 January, he called for the dissolution of the Junta Patriótica and set up 'public order units' designed to control and contain the popular explosion. At the same time, negotiations began to create a political agreement between AD, COPEI (a Christian Democratic organisation in origin) and the much smaller URD (Democratic Republican Union), led by Ojeda. In October 1958 the three organisations signed a pact at Punto Fijo; it was to determine the shape of Venezuelan politics for the next 40 years.

Essentially, the Punto Fijo Accord was a power-sharing agreement between the two major parties, hidden behind the creation of a national government. In the period between January and October there were several more military risings, both from the right and from the left, though it was Hugo Trejo's group of 170 officers which posed the most serious threat. Revolutionary committees were formed in many barrios in combination with armed brigades of workers and community activists. AD's response was to mobilise its supporters against these manifestations of a revolutionary impulse. And it found support from the Communist Party, perhaps because of its expectation of inclusion in a new AD government – a hope which would be disappointed. But in the crucial ideological battles of the time, the Communist Party's decision weakened the left and strengthened AD at a critical moment. Thus, when elections were held on 7 December 1958, it was AD and its leader Betancourt that emerged the victors.

Acción Democrática was more than simply a political party. Like the Congress Party of India or the Mexican PRI (Institutional Revolutionary Party), AD was a machinery of power, patronage and social and political control. Once in the state it became the state, distributing favours to the functionaries of a bloated state machine not simply at the national level, but at every level of politics. State governors were not elected until 1989, for example, but selected from an official list – and permanent jobs were within the gift of the coalition parties, but mainly AD, and were distributed in exchange for electoral and political support. All this was made possible by a consensus on oil. Venezuela was now fully an oil producer; oil was responsible for close to 90 per cent of its export earnings. It was also determining in a wider sense. The continuing mass influx of rural migrants to the precarious hillside shanty towns around the cities represented a systematic abandonment of the countryside and produced a dramatic decline in agricultural production – an agriculture which until the discovery of 'the devil's excrement' as Pérez Alfonso described oil, had earned most of Venezuela's GDP. Although Venezuela's share of oil profits was paltry, the volume of earnings was more than sufficient to sustain a bloated and corrupt bureaucracy with an enormous appetite for consumption and much less for productive work. When the oil price rose, there would be enough over to distribute additional crumbs to the majority population, in the form of free education, a health system and jobs in the service sector. The Punto Fijo agreement allowed for regular elections, in which the two main parties alternated; they were properly and cleanly conducted – since no rival could possibly challenge their duopoly. This earned Venezuela its reputation as an exemplary democracy in a region where they were rare. And Rómulo Betancourt became its representative figure.

In fact Betancourt quickly discarded his progressive mask. Initially a supporter of the Cuban Revolution of 1959, his government very soon turned against demonstrating unemployed workers and the growing Campaign for the Right to Bread. AD split over these decisions, with the left forming the MIR (Movement of the Revolutionary Left) while Fabricio Ojeda's URD left the government in protest against the government's support for sanctions against Cuba. The urban rebellion continued into September and October 1960. And when the oil price fell, early in 1961, Betancourt introduced savage emergency economic measures, seeking foreign loans and reducing public sector wages. The supply of crumbs had suddenly dried up! By the following year the pretence of liberal democracy had been abandoned internally, but externally Betancourt continued to be seen as a model democrat, overseeing a smooth parliamentary process and a rational economic policy. What people outside Venezuela did not see was the repression he unleashed, which would be continued by his successor, the 'grandfatherly' Raúl Leoni.

The insurrectionary mood of 1960 affected both urban and rural movements. Land occupations proliferated and, according to Douglas Bravo,[9] seven armed cells or focos were already operating in Caracas alone. At the same time, opposition currents inside the army were growing; Trejo's involvement in the overthrow of Pérez Jiménez both expressed and encouraged their development, and two military rebellions in 1962 would underline their political significance. The Cuban Revolution of 1 January 1959 and the rapid unmasking of Betancourt after 1958 generated a debate across the Venezuelan left that continued in one form or another until the end of the century. Its central question was how to forge a 'civic-military alliance', building on the organs of mass resistance that had emerged during and after the overthrow of Pérez Jiménez, and on the growing opposition within the armed forces.

What did emerge in the face of Betancourt's fierce repression was an armed guerrilla movement in which Bravo was to play a central role. In the tense atmosphere of late 1960 a number of military personnel offered to join the guerrilla detachments – and a number did, though others returned to barracks to await a more promising moment. Betancourt's systematic anti-guerrilla operation continued, however, dividing the country into eight 'operational zones', each with their own commander, to conduct a relentless counter-guerrilla campaign. There was a history of rural resistance in Venezuela extending back to the 1930s, and the Venezuelan Communist Party had taken part in the creation of indigenous armed resistance groups before 1960. But the Cuban example spurred sections of the left to adopt a guerrilla strategy in the face of mounting repression. In March 1961, having previously supported Betancourt despite his explicit and militant anti-communism, the congress of the Communist Party opted for armed struggle. Douglas Bravo, who until then had taken responsibility for trade union work, was now designated to take charge of the party's armed section. Guerrilla fronts were formed in Falcón and Lara provinces as well as Yaracuy, and a number of the students involved in the confrontations in the universities late in 1960 now joined them. In May 1962 two military rebellions, at the naval base at Carúpano and a month later at Puerto Cabello did attract some degree of civilian support, particularly the second. But it was clear by then that the mass movement was in retreat, especially after a crackdown on the transport strike in Táchira province at the end of the previous year. The sustained counter-guerrilla operation was claiming huge numbers, among them the 76 guerrilla fighters put on trial in November that year among many thousands of arrested and detained opponents of the regime, including the charismatic Fabricio Ojeda who had joined the guerrillas in Lara but was then arrested in October.[10]

The formation of the Armed Forces of National Liberation (FALN) in 1963, under the command of Douglas Bravo, coincided with a retreat in the popular movement, as Bravo himself acknowledges. The central government was relentless in its pursuit of the guerrillas, although their resistance continued – invariably at a high human cost. In 1965, the Communist Party withdrew its support for the guerrilla struggle and expelled Bravo when he refused to accept the decision. He then formed his own organisation, the Party of the Venezuelan Revolution (PRV).

The fractures and splits that characterised the politics of the Venezuelan left in the late 1960s and early 1970s are too many and too Jesuitical to follow in any detail. But they address in their insistently detailed ways the same fundamental issues and raise the same questions. What are the social forces that can successfully oppose a state with the considerable resources that the oil industry provided, and what methods and strategies can create the instruments of struggle that can resist both sustained repression and the slow ethical erosion that corruption and an immovable political system encourage? How could organs of coordination and unified leadership develop when the prevailing forms of radical resistance in that period had emerged at the grassroots and in largely local conditions, and under the influence of political ideas that laid stress on autonomy and were generally suspicious of political parties – unsurprisingly given their history of splits and cooptation? The very public split between Douglas Bravo and Fidel Castro in 1969 came in response to the definitive abandonment of the guerrilla strategy by Castro in the wake of Che's failed Bolivian expedition and his death. In Bravo's view, Cuba was now serving Soviet interests in the region, and a continuing armed struggle could only represent an obstacle to the Communist Parties' search for political allies and opportunities in Latin America. Hence, according to Bravo, Cuba's pursuit of united fronts with non-revolutionary forces at the expense of the Latin American revolution.

The political atmosphere into which Hugo Chávez made his cautious way in the early 1970s was shaped by these events and by that history. While Bravo remained an advocate of armed struggle, and refused the amnesty offered by the new government of Rafael Caldera in 1969, his strategic idea had developed and expanded beyond the guerrilla warfare strategy advocated by Guevara on the back of the Cuban Revolution. Bravo had, after all, experienced the isolation and persecution of the guerrilla groups by the exemplary democratic governments of Betancourt and Leoni. And in his rethinking of revolutionary strategy in the specific conditions of Venezuela he had built on his reading of the independence revolutions led by Bolívar – and saw the revolutionary movement of the late twentieth century as historically continuous with those earlier struggles. Philosophically, he was evolving a fusion of Marxism and the politics of class struggle with a radical nationalism associated with the name of Simón Bolívar. Chávez and Bravo would meet later and develop an intense political relationship around some shared ideas, before Chávez broke with Bravo for reasons to which we shall return.

What is significant is that the political crises and conflicts of the late 1960s produced a range of alternative strategies and arguments. The amnesty offered by Caldera in 1969, for example, provided an opportunity for a number of leaders of the guerrilla movement to abandon class struggle politics in favour of varieties of reformism, the pursuit of change within the existing system. The most prominent of those who took this position was Teodoro Petkoff, the guerrilla leader who founded the Movement Toward Socialism (MAS) and would later become both an advocate of neo-liberal economic solutions and a bitter enemy of Chávez. Another current led by the influential and much-admired intellectual Alfredo Maneiro formed Causa R, with a more explicitly based class politics based on working-class organisation. Its strength, and its social base, was in Bolívar province, around the cities of Ciudad Guayana and Puerto Ordaz, site of Venezuela's most important industrial plants, the steel industry complex SIDOR and the aluminium processing plant, Alcasa.

The Rise and Fall of Saudi Venezuela

The Acción Democrática governments of the 1960s had successfully beaten back the political challenges mounted by the guerrillas and the mass resistance from below: and it had done so from two directions. The sophisticated and ruthless machinery of repression claimed an estimated 3,000 opponents tortured and killed in secret operations in this much-praised exemplary democracy, with its regular and clean presidential elections. The system worked well in its allocation of posts and distribution of favours between the two major parties – Acción Democrática and Copei – and their alternation in power. The Punto Fijo agreement, rooted in a shared hostility to communism expressed in the original, significantly named, Waldorf Astoria Agreement that predated Punto Fijo, had produced 'an oil state integrated into the geo-strategic conceptions of a western world headed by the United States'. In this state, the political parties acted as what Bravo describes as a 'kind of holding company', containing and controlling every aspect of social and economic life and distributing the wealth generated by oil among a privileged layer who maintained the machinery of power in their own, and their masters' interests, administering and distributing wealth and power without any regard to its equitable allocation across the whole of society. It is a strange democracy indeed that is concerned only with electoral mechanics while sustaining a broader social system of embedded inequality.

This growth of a marginal population around and within the cities was provoking a deeper crisis – Bravo calls it 'the other crisis' – at once social, economic and psychological. An economy dependent entirely on oil for its income ceases to foment production elsewhere and replace it with imports.[11] The small, skilled working class that extracts and distributes the oil is a privileged elite held down by its relatively privileged position within the working class. The bloated management structures of a state and an oil industry which coexist at this stage in parallel but separate worlds, shelter and maintain a social layer distinguished by its patterns of consumption and its essentially parasitic nature – it is the members of that layer who enunciate that catchphrase of the Venezuelan middle class at this time – 'its cheap give me two' (*Tá barato dame dos*). And even if things are not actually cheaper than their domestic equivalents, the dominant culture in oil-producing societies mimics the patterns of western consumption, whose norms and ideals are invariably 'made in America'. The population of Maracaibo, for example, where oil was first discovered and which remains a key oil-producing region, considers itself to be a separate country and names its children in ways that underline the fact that they feel closer to the US than to the rest of Venezuela.

In this way, politics was debased and caricatured in its turn, reduced to an exchange of favours and privileges in a cycle of corruption that penetrates every level of social life. This is what the Venezuelan poor meant when they spoke of political parties – which from their point of view were mere mechanisms of exclusion, maintaining them – and with them their history and their culture, their songs and dances, at the margins in areas reserved for the primitive and the backward: essentially, in permanent exclusion. But they were not blind to the huge gas-guzzling cars careering up and down the grand avenues that were Pérez Jiménez's legacy. And while the plush restaurants and whisky-drinking culture of Altamira and all points east in Caracas were not available to them, they knew they were there.

This 'other crisis' reached perhaps its most obscene moments in 1973–74, the era known as 'Saudi Venezuela'. The combination of the Yom Kippur War and the oil crisis that followed brought a massive boom in oil prices. Venezuela splashed its wealth around the world; its students abroad enjoyed huge grants, its civil servants lived out their most extravagant dreams. This enormous rush of wealth still represented only the absurdly low royalties paid by the multinational oil giants who controlled Venezuela's oil. Yet it did reinforce the notion that the oil never ends, and deepened dependency.

Carlos Andrés Pérez, President of Venezuela, was the man who had presented Hugo Chávez with his sabre when he graduated from the military academy in 1974. The recently elected president, known usually by his initials CAP, was enjoying a wave of popularity as booming oil prices allowed him to make extravagant promises of forthcoming great leaps forward and that he would 'sembrar el petróleo', sow the seeds of oil and harvest them by investing in a range of social projects to benefit the majority. His own humble background and his charismatic public persona, together with the unprecedently high price of oil, made him seem credible at the time. And the nationalisation of the oil corporation in 1976 gave him additional credibility. But it is now widely acknowledged that this was a fraudulent nationalisation (*una nacionalización chucuta*) in which the Venezuelan state assumed responsibility for infrastructural investment while the multinationals continued to benefit from national oil production through a complex and labyrinthine set of interconnecting operating agreements. In addition, the national oil corporation Pdvsa began to invest heavily in refineries and petrol stations abroad, buying the Citgo chain in the US, whose profits were rarely directly repatriated but instead disappeared into a maze of offshore companies run by the company's executives. And it very soon became clear that while the expected income fell well short of what was anticipated, CAP had covered himself by acquiring loans from international agencies which, at this time of prosperity, raised Venezuela's national debt to new levels and actually depressed the living standards of the majority.

As Hugo Chávez prepared to leave the Military Academy for his first posting, this was the Venezuela he would encounter. The individual qualities of this young military officer from the llanos, his impulse to recapture a history of resistance and struggle which had been, for a long time, appropriated by the Venezuelan elite as their own, his sympathy and identification with the poor majority and his ability to communicate that sympathy in effective and credible ways, his revulsion at injustice and at the corruption of the rulers of his nation and his interpretation of his duty as a soldier as one of service to his own country, are not in question. But to explain his outstanding role in its history, we have to make sense of the circumstances and conditions of the first decade of the twenty-first century, which allowed those qualities both to develop and to influence to such an extraordinary degree the history not just of Venezuela, but of Latin America as a whole.

2

The Dream of Simón Bolívar

Within a month of his graduation, in 1975, Chávez was given his first assignment. He was put in charge of communications in a counter-guerrilla detachment dispatched to his home state of Barinas. The once active guerrilla movement was now largely beaten, leaving only a small number still dedicated to armed struggle. It was a particularly unpropitious moment for the surviving guerrillas, with Venezuela's economic boom at its height. In fact Chávez had very little actual fighting to do. Instead he worked on local radio and, so legend has it, started a study group using Marxist texts he found in a burned-out car that had been used by some fleeing guerrillas. He clearly made himself popular with the local inhabitants, organising events celebrating local culture and writing a witty weekly column in the local newspaper *El Espacio*. Inevitably there are suggestions that he was already discussing his political ambitions with friends and colleagues. More substantially, he wrote in his diary that: 'My people are stoical, passive. Who will light the flame? We could raise a fire but the wood is wet. The conditions aren't right. The conditions aren't there. Blast it! When will they exist, or can we create them? Subjectively, the conditions are right, but not objectively. It's a great excuse'[1]

It's a slightly grandiose entry, and it is less than clear who the comment at the end of the entry is directed at. Clearly people were talking politics and the standard theme of political discussion – corruption – never ceased to be a topic of interest. What is clear is that Chávez was restless and not a little frustrated. His unit belonged to the battalion created to persecute and destroy guerrillas, and he will have been familiar with the ideological defence of its activities from the classes on the topic at the Academy. But the absence of a visible enemy will have given him time to reflect on the nature of the enterprise. At the same time, his active contacts with local communities, his activities on radio and in the press, and his tendency to organise sporting and other events seemed more in keeping with an idea of the role of the military he associated with the military reformers like Torrijos and Velasco, whom he had studied.

At 22 his ideas were only in formation, though the constant thread running through his thoughts and writings is Bolívar, together with Zamora and Rodríguez, the other heroes of the independence struggle. He makes another pointed comment in his diary about baseball – his first great love – noting that like so many other cultural products it is North American, not local. This observation is part of his increasing irritation with the ubiquitous presence of the US in every area of Venezuelan life; economic, political, cultural. 'We are lacking an identity', was his final comment.

In 1977, still only 23, Chávez married a local girl, Nancy Colmenares; she was carrying his first child, a daughter. Chávez's mother Elena always disapproved of Nancy, perhaps because of her humble background or her lack of ambition. Elena had aspirations for her son. But Hugo was not about to settle down into provincial domestic life. An incident he reported in Barcelona (Venezuela), where he was sent to gather supplies, is significant. While there he saw a senior officer beating three presumed guerrillas; Chávez intervened and stopped him, at the risk of severe sanctions for contradicting and attacking a senior officer. As Chávez later reported to the writer Gabriel García Márquez when they shared a return flight from Havana, he began to ask himself, 'Why am I here? On the one hand there are peasants in uniform torturing peasant guerrilla fighters. On the other peasant guerrillas are murdering peasants in uniform. The war was over. It didn't make any sense any more to be shooting anybody.'[2]

He had also been sent, a little earlier, to suppress a guerrilla rising in Cumana province led by the mysterious ultra-left grouping Bandera Roja (Red Flag). But when he returned home that Christmas (1977), he confided in his brother Adán, always a key political influence on him, his increasing unease with his position in the military.

It was a strange and contradictory position Chávez found himself in, but not one confined to him. Armies are not voluntary institutions. In a command structure, and whatever their sympathies, individual soldiers are expected to carry out the tasks assigned to them – and are punished if they do not. Those tasks are determined by the state the military serves. For a soldier who has come to question those interests the options are to break with the institution, with all the sanctions that that implies, or to wait for (or to work for) the collapse of the institution itself. Inescapably, that will involve leading a double life.

As far as Chávez knew, his brother was a member of the MIR – the left split from Acción Democrática which had for a period joined Douglas Bravo's guerrillas in the FALN.[3] In fact, Adán Chávez was a member of Bravo's organisation the PRV, and shared its vision of a revolutionary Bolivarianism. He later introduced his brother to Douglas Bravo and others who would play a critical role in Chávez's political development. But their conversations resolved one issue for Hugo. He had said to Adán that he was thinking of retiring from the army and looking for a teaching position, perhaps even at Adán's university, the University of the Andes in Merida, the beautiful city nestling in the high Andes. Adán dissuaded him. It was important, he argued, to have radicals embedded in the military and agitating among other soldiers and sailors and airmen.

What lay behind Adán's advice was a deeper, strategic idea that Bravo had begun to elaborate after a profound self-criticism about the guerrilla strategy and its failure to resist state repression. Bravo himself had a wide range of contacts within the army. He had cousins who were soldiers – but then, as he said, almost everyone had relatives in the army, precisely because of its relatively democratic character in the sense that it recruited from every layer of Venezuelan society. The overthrow of Pérez Jiménez had involved a number of military people, in particular the group around Hugo Trejo. And in the wake of Pérez 's overthrow, Bravo had been appointed by the Communist Party to develop contacts with the military, though it also already had a specific internal commission to build organisation within the armed forces. The number of dissident officers with connections to organisations of the left increased in the early 1960s. The rebellions at the naval bases of Carúpano and Puerto Cabello had produced a number of recruits for the guerrillas as state repression increased; but both had occurred at a time when the wider mass movement was in retreat, for the same reasons, though the Puerto Cabello rising had involved a number of civilians. Many of the military participants then joined the guerrillas.

The political lessons that Bravo drew from the experience of the 1960s was that the subject of future social risings would be an alliance of forces, both civilian and military. The 'civic–military alliance' that he proposed drew in the grassroots organs of resistance that continued to grow up, particularly in the poorer areas, despite the ferocious attempts to destroy them, and the radicals and dissenters within the army, as well as the emerging liberation theology movement which was especially active in the barrios. Adán Chávez and Douglas Bravo clearly saw a role for Hugo in recruiting his military colleagues to the cause. And it was equally important that an organisation that was avowedly Marxist and revolutionary, like Bravo's PRV, had also embraced Bolívar and revolutionary nationalism. It was almost certainly that combination that convinced and moved Hugo Chávez into the next phase of his now overtly political career.

Hugo Chávez's physical encounter with Bravo, which would in many ways be a turning point, in fact came later. But the die was cast. A short time after the incident with the violent Colonel – and with the customary luck that allowed him to avoid harsher sanctions – Chávez was sent to Maturín, where he met with his fellow *llanero* and companion in conspiracy for the next decade, Jesús Urdaneta Hernández, together with two other young officers, Miguel Ortiz Contreras and Felipe Acosta Carles. They formed their first clandestine group, the Popular Liberation Army of Venezuela (EPRV). Despite its name, which echoed many of Latin America's guerrilla groupings, it was not seen as the nucleus of a guerrilla army. Chávez was clear in his own mind that the guerrilla strategy was no longer an option, and indeed most guerrilla fighters were by now dead or had abandoned armed struggle for other political methods. That was a conclusion that led him, logically enough, to seek a meeting with Alfredo Maneiro, himself an ex-communist guerrilla and the charismatic leader of Causa R, an organisation which would have considerable weight in Venezuela and educate many leading activists supporting Chávez in government.

Maneiro's political philosophy began with a critical appraisal of political parties and their impact. He argued instead for the building of a movement, linking existing struggles, in which 'the masses themselves would decide on their own political direction'. 'Instead of starting with a given political structure, it was important to trust in the capacity of the popular movement to take on the task of producing a new leadership from within its own ranks.'[4]

Maneiro therefore concentrated on three areas of active social struggle. The Central University in Caracas was and continues to be the site of regular confrontation with government – partly because the tradition of university autonomy in Latin America theoretically prevents government from intervening directly on campuses. In reality successive governments have closed or otherwise contained the university on a number of occasions. The second area where Causa R worked systematically was Catia, a working class area of Caracas – of some half a million inhabitants – which was well known for its collective spirit of resistance. Many prominent political leaders grew up in the area, among them the current president Nicolás Maduro.

The third area of strength, and ultimately the social base of Causa R over subsequent decades, was the workers movement in the main industrial area around Ciudad Guyana in the east of the country. Here Sidor, the massive steel-making complex built by Pérez Jiménez, was the heartland of a trade union movement which had become more militant in the wake of a long strike in 1972. The key workers leaders of Causa R, Pablo Medina and Andrés Velásquez, were both based there and became prominent political figures throughout the 1980s – indeed Velásquez was twice elected governor of Bolívar state, where Ciudad Guyana is located. He later won an impressive 22 per cent of the vote in the 1993 presidential elections.

Hard though it is to imagine it of a man of his legendary loquacity, Chávez said barely a word throughout their one-hour interview. (They did not meet again before Maneiro's untimely death in 1982.) In 1978, Chávez was sent to Maracay, where he was promoted to lieutenant, and where his fascination with tanks led him to seek, and win, a transfer to the tank regiment based there.

The EPRV continued to meet conspiratorially, and the four original participants formed a nucleus around which other officers could gather to discuss Venezuela's now worsening situation. The very ostentatious corruption of Carlos Andres Pérez's government did not stop at the barrack gates, and the younger officers of poorer backgrounds, like the members of the EPRV, were shocked by the theft of public funds by the upper echelons of the army and their extravagant lifestyles. At the same time, they were not shut off from the impact of the deepening economic crisis that followed the short lived boom of Saudi Venezuela. By the time CAP (Pérez) handed over the presidency in 1979, he was just in time to escape a kickback scandal that was knocking on his door. Corruption, inefficiency, poor management, and extravagant spending on vanity projects exacerbated a crisis that was threatening as the skyhigh oil prices began to fall. It was the case that there had been high levels of public spending in education and health in the 1970s. The new president, Luis Herrera Campins (1979–84), whose campaign slogan was 'Where has all the money gone', tried to deal with the crisis by cutting public spending and beginning a process of privatisation. And his successor, Jaime Lusinchi (1984–89), introduced still harsher measures while at the same time exemplifying the endemic corruption of the system by leaving most of the decisions to his secretary and lover Blanca Ibáñez.[5]

The group of young radical officers were far closer to the realities of life for the majority of Venezuelans than their high living officers. They knew first hand that unemployment levels were rising and that the shortlived benefits of the boom decade were rapidly being eroded by inflation. And Chávez himself was moving closer to the most dramatic areas of conflict. In 1980 he was moved to Caracas to teach history and sports at the military academy. Either the military authorities were blissfully unaware of the political activity, or they chose to bring Chávez closer in order to control him. Or perhaps they were just keen to get him out of Maracay and away from his tank regiment, a dangerous instrument in the hands of a rebel!

Of course, Chávez was by no means alone in his secret organising. William Izarra returned from a year at Harvard in 1978 to rejoin the air force. His R-83 (the 83 referred to the year that foreign oil contracts were scheduled to end), formed in 1979, was actively organising among his fellow commissioned and non-commissioned officers. And although he was in regular contact with Chávez, his perspective was more clearly socialist. His view of Venezuelan democracy was that it was so corrupt and controlled by networks of patronage and clientilism that it could not be removed at the ballot box. Instead, it would be overthrown by a movement of civilian organisations and the radical military, the 'civic-military alliance' which Douglas Bravo was advocating. The tinder, it seemed, was beginning to dry out.

In Caracas, Chávez's ebullient personality, his charismatic teaching style and his profound knowledge of Venezuela's history were winning him a reputation and a growing number of supporters. And he was now meeting regularly with Douglas Bravo. In 1983, after a rally to commemorate Bolívar, Chávez and his earlier collaborators gathered again to form a new conspiracy – the Bolivarian Revolutionary Movement (MBR-200).[6] In Richard Gott's view,[7] it was more a political study group than the embryo of a political party. But they were certainly discussing active subversion, and their Bolivarianism was permeated by revolutionary ideas – although Chávez said nothing to his fellow subversives about his meetings with Bravo. Bravo was a well known communist, and the Bolivarians were deeply divided over their attitude to the Marxist revolutionaries – their revolution would be Bolivarian and nationalist.

The four original members of the EPRV, now joined by Raúl Isaías Baduel, jogged together to the Samán de Guere, the wide spreading tree near Maracay under which Simón Bolívar had rested to reflect during several of his campaigns, and there they repeated his famous oath of 1805: 'I swear before you, and I swear before the god of my fathers, that I will not allow my arm to relax, nor my soul to rest, until I have broken the chains that oppress us ... .'

The members of William Izarra's R-83 also swore an oath of allegiance under the shadow of Bolívar – in their case at the Pantheon in Caracas where he was buried.

What unified the revolutionaries, therefore, was their shared commitment to continuing the liberation process that Bolívar had embarked on two centuries earlier, which Simón Rodríguez and Ezequiel Zamora had driven forward in their turn, and which Hugo Chávez, like his fellow conspirators, was committed to complete.

Their planned rising, whenever it came, would be Bolivarian. It would owe nothing to earlier revolutions – the Russian, Chinese, even the Cuban, despite Chávez's admiration for Fidel Castro, which was to increase over the years. The MBR brought together people with different understandings of the Bolivarian revolution, but as long as their reference point was Bolívar's struggle for independence, there could be agreement among its members. At a later stage their differences would emerge and produce divisions within the movement.

The Ideals of Bolívar

The image of Simón Bolívar as a national symbol had been squabbled over by every political camp, much like Marti in Cuba. The difference now was that Bolívar was rediscovered, by the MBR-200 among others, as a guide to contemporary social movements for change. There are several Bolívars – or at least different visions of how he saw the achievement of national independence, and what it meant.

The origins of Bolívar's thinking were in a Rousseauian vision – the defence of individual liberty and equality within a framework of restraints that guaranteed the social order. The republic he envisaged would have a strong and centralised state in which three different institutions would oversee and check one another – a legislature elected under universal suffrage, a hereditary Senate, and a body of appointed Censors, the elders of the community to mediate between the other forces. Over time a re-educated people would be able to exercise responsible direct control; but in the context of a Latin America emerging from three centuries of Spanish imperial domination, the conflict between rival powers for control endangered the stability of the new republics. For Bolívar, then, the central actor, the subject, of history was the nation breaking free of external domination. This is the background to Bolívar's famous *Letter from Jamaica*, written in 1815 from exile after three years of independence wars. In reality it was a veiled appeal for British support for Latin American Independence against the Spanish empire.

Bolívar was born in Caracas in 1783 into a wealthy aristocratic family. His parents died when he was very young and he was placed under the guidance of several tutors, the most influential of whom was Simón Rodríguez, a revolutionary who introduced his young pupil not only to the landscapes of his country, but to the ideas of the Enlightenment, of Rousseau and Voltaire. At 14 his radical guide was forced into exile for conspiring against Spain, and Simón was left in charge of 'the only father I ever had', his legendary black maid La Negra Hipólita. A year later he entered the military academy, before embarking, like any young man of his station, on a Grand Tour of Europe. In 1802, he married the young Spanish aristocrat María Teresa Rodríguez del Toro. She died of yellow fever in 1804, on the couple's first visit to Latin America. Bolívar was heartbroken and never remarried, though his reputation as a very active lover suggested he did not live his life alone, even before meeting the fiercely loyal companion of his later years Manuela Sáenz.

He returned to Caracas in 1807, enthused by the revolutionary ideas he had seen at work in Europe. Napoleon's invasion of Spain undermined her imperial role; its empire was visibly crumbling and Bolívar returned full of optimism about the possibilities of Latin American independence. But his hopes found little echo in his own class and he returned to working his estates in Yare. Under the imperial monopoly of trade, the colonies were restricted in what they could cultivate and what they could (or could not) manufacture. But the landholding class had no sympathy with the European Enlightenment in general, and still less with the proposed end to slavery, all the more after the slave revolt in Coro in 1795. In fact the French National Assembly had already reneged on its promise to end slavery long before Napoleon conquered the Iberian Peninsula in 1808. In Caracas, the landed classes created their own government in 1810, not to defy Spain but to conserve the imperial structures until Spanish regal control was re-established. Bolívar himself took no part in the the new regime – he disapproved. Nevertheless he was sent to London to negotiate on its behalf with the British government, where he was received in London by Francisco de Miranda; he was much older than Bolívar, had experienced the French Revolution and was a passionate advocate of its values and ideals. For that very reason the fiery revolutionary was regarded with deep suspicion by the creole elites. But they were unable to prevent his return with (or shortly after) Bolívar at the end of that year.

In July 1811, the Battle of Carabobo marked a definitive defeat for Spain; in December that year the newly established ruling council published the first constitution of the new Venezuelan Republic. Then in March 1812 an earthquake devastated Caracas, but when it was suggested to Bolívar that God and Nature were enemies of the new Venezuela, he famously declared that Nature too could be defeated. The new Constitution promised liberty, equality, property and security, but it did not liberate the slaves nor extend the franchise beyond the propertied classes. And it conceded various degrees of autonomy to the regions. In Bolívar's view, this meant that the new Republic was born with fatal flaws, compromising the central power; and its promise of equality without abolition was empty. The black slaves erupted in insurrection, and the conservative anti-independence forces exploited their anger to further confuse the situation. The new nation sank into in-fighting and Bolívar left for Cartagena; there he issued what was in effect his first key political document, the Cartagena Manifesto. Bolívar had come of age and a steely determination now replaced his earlier self-doubt. He assembled a force of 200 men and overwhelmed the Spanish outpost of Santa Marta; his victory speech to the small group on the river bank, however, was designed for a much larger audience. He fought his way through Nueva Granada to the Venezuelan border, which gave him authority in its Congress to argue for an invasion of Venezuela under his leadership. The internal situation in Venezuela was anarchic and the pro-royalist forces were acting with extreme brutality. Bolívar responded by warning 'Our hatred will be implacable, the war will be to the death'.[8] This 'Admirable Campaign' ended with Bolívar's triumphal entry into Caracas in August 1813 where he declared: 'I have come to bring you the rule of law. Military despotism cannot ensure the happiness of a people. A victorious soldier acquires no right to rule his country ... I am a simple citizen, and the general will of the people shall always be for me the supreme law.'[9]

Yet within a year, Bolívar was in flight from the relentless advance of the white and black armies led by the bloodthirsty *caudillo* from the plains, José Tomás Boves. He sailed for Cartagena again, and later summarised the moment in his 1816 *Letter from Jamaica*.

The concession to federalism, he argued, sowed inevitable seeds of fracture and internal conflict as local interests prevailed over the general good. An inexperienced nation could not forge its own identity until the people were mature enough; in the meantime, power would have to be centralised, not in a monarch, but in a president for life. The struggle for independence, he noted, had brought death and destruction, a million dead and the chaos of warring local interests in a disunited region still run by tyrants, although, as he put it 'they govern a desert'. The key to the future of independent nations, to which he remained uncompromisingly committed, was integration and unity under a leader who would govern according to the highest liberal values and in defence of the general good.

In 1819, Venezuela achieved full independence. From then on, Bolívar devoted himself to the creation of the Greater Colombia he had always dreamed of. His military and human exploits in achieving that, in 1824, are legendary – and extraordinary. And they provide a kind of historical narrative in which Chávez saw parallels with the present. The column of ill-clad plainsmen Bolívar led over the High Andes, in inhuman conditions, allowed him to outflank the Spanish troops and defeat them at the Battle of Boyacá. Named as President of Venezuela in 1819 and of Gran Colombia in 1821, he marched on through Ecuador to Peru, where Congress declared him President in 1824. In December, at the battle of Ayacucho, the inspired young general Sucre defeated the Spanish in freezing conditions. Peru was conquered, and early in 1825, Bolívar and Sucre set out for the final prize – Upper Peru, or Bolivia as it would soon be named, after the Liberator.

And yet, in 1826, the constitution he wrote for the country that had taken his name and acknowledged his unique and overwhelming impact on a newly independent Latin America expressed ideas very different from those he had presented to the Congress of Angostura, when he had accepted the presidency of the new Venezuela. Then he had said, 'The continuation of authority in the same individual has frequently meant the end of democratic governments. Repeated elections are essential in proper systems of government.' In Bolivia

Figure 3.1 3D reconstruction of the face of Bolívar, 'The Liberator' (*El Arañero/Pdvsa*)

he had decreed the return of indigenous lands to their people and the abolition of slavery; yet he told the British consul in La Paz that 'my heart always beats in favour of liberty, but my head leans towards aristocracy ... if the principles of liberty are too rapidly introduced, anarchy and the destruction of the white inhabitants will be the inevitable consequences.'[10] In the four years that followed Bolívar would be betrayed, defrauded, abandoned and threatened, until his ignominious death from tuberculosis in December 1830.[11] As he was dying he was heard to say 'America is ungovernable. Those who served the revolution have ploughed the sea'.[12]

On his journey to Bolivia, Bolívar was accompanied by his tutor, Simón Rodríguez (or Robinson as he periodically called himself), who had been a defining influence on his early years. His insistence on the rights of indigenous people and his lacerating comments about colonialism and the inept *criollos* won him the enmity of the deeply conservative Bolivian ruling class. In his later years he worked as an educator in Chile. But for Hugo Chávez, who resurrected the virtually forgotten Robinson for the later twentieth century, he represented the radical ideas – on integration and unity, on equality and social justice, and on the necessity of revolution – that he would argue were the essence of Bolivarianism.[13]

Bolívar in the Age of Oil

Every political force in Venezuela, and many in Latin America, claimed Bolívar for their own. He was a heroic figure, romantic, and in some sense above politics. He represented the nation – but he also concealed its divisions and contradictions. The debate around his ideas and significance often centred on his later writings and speeches and the disillusionment that led him increasingly to emphasize the critical role of the leader. The emphasis that Chávez laid in his understanding of the Liberator was different, in the sense that he placed the radical Simón Rodríguez, who had described himself as a socialist, at the centre of his interpretation.

What was beyond question was Bolívar's lifelong dedication to national liberation, though from the outset he saw the survival of new nations emerging from colonialism as contingent on their integration into a greater unity – his Gran Colombia. In the century after his early death, as the endless array of statues, busts and portraits show, he was above all a military leader, a great general, a master tactician – all of which of course were true. But the struggle for national liberation succeeds to the extent that it releases social forces. The invisible armies, the hundreds of thousands who died in these long and exhausting struggles – the million dead that Bolívar cited in his Jamaica Letter for example – were indigenous people, black slaves, mixed-race *pardos* in his own Venezuela, each fighting not simply as followers of Bolívar's great vision but in the expectation that national liberation would fulfil their dreams and aspirations. Bolívar clearly felt that the internal conflicts within the movement, as well as personal rivalries and ambitions, had threatened the project of national sovereignty.

The Bolívar that Chávez celebrated and paid homage to in his new movement was a soldier, a fighter for national self-emancipation and an anti-imperialist – though in the latter case there are ambiguities to be recognised in Bolívar's own actions. But beyond the symbolic historical figure, what was the significance of Bolívar for Chávez and his group? At one level, the Bolivarian aspect of MBR's revolutionary thinking derived directly from one aspect of Bolívar's ideas and writings – his emphasis on the specificity of Latin American experience and his resistance to a mechanical application of European ideas to a continent trapped in economic and ideological backwardness and still dominated by a local creole ruling class profoundly attached to the structures of the imperial arrangement. At the same time, regional and sectional interests exercised a deeply destructive influence, acting directly against the unity of the prospective nation. And Bolívar was clear on the economic realities surrounding the struggle for independence. While Latin America's colonial history left it with an economy producing primary materials for Europe, it was unable to fulfil even its minimum domestic needs.

José Revenga, Bolívar's close economic adviser pointed to 'the excessive import' of many articles which were previously produced by poor families here:

> Foreign soap, for example, has destroyed the various soap factories which we formerly had in the interior. And now we even take candles from abroad, retailed at eight per *real*. The few that are still made in this country import their wick from abroad ... It is striking that the more we rely on foreign interests to supply our needs, the more we diminish our national independence and our reliance now even extends to daily and vital needs.[14]

With the addition of the word 'oil', these comments become chillingly contemporary.

Bolívar was also a soldier fascinated by tactics and fieldcraft. Chávez describes his own growing fascination with military skills. Within the MBR there was a tension which became increasingly present in the secret meetings in houses and apartments around the country, which later – as the group expanded – were recast as congresses of the MBR.[15] The group, unlike earlier groupings Chávez had formed, was now explicitly involved in preparing for an insurrection. This development almost certainly had to do with the changing external circumstances. 1983 was the year of 'Black Friday' the collapse of Venezuela's banking sector in a morass of corruption and incompetence. But the crisis was a reflection of the deep indebtedness of the Venezuelan state, the wild speculation fuelled by the rising oil prices of the 1970s, and the public and private loans contracted by state agencies and private enterprises, mainly for purposes of speculation. As the price of oil fell, the bubble burst, and the cutbacks in public spending, attacks on living standards, and the severe blow taken by the middle class that watched as its current accounts disappeared overnight, were signs of things to come. The complacency of the 1970s, the naive belief that the boom would last for ever, certainly sustained by Carlos Andrés Pérez's bombastic self-confidence, made that a lean time for revolutionary ideas. But when the cracks began to show, the abuses of power and the public purse that were common knowledge rose to the surface. As popular discontent rose, to pursue Chávez's metaphor, the tinder dried out in the grate.

The MBR were not untouched by the debate on the left about organisation and political method. Chávez had been extremely impressed by Afredo Maneiro of Causa R when they met in 1978 – dumbstruck in fact! He would take up the relationship again, with Maneiro's successor, Pablo Medina, in 1983. But before that he had come under the influence of the charismatic Douglas Bravo. They met in 1980, at Bravo's instigation. Bravo had throughout his career laid emphasis on the role of radicals in the armed forces as part of the civic–military alliance. Many had joined his guerrilla forces, but now he recognised that the guerrilla strategy was not appropriate for building this kind of broad fighting organisation. This was not to say that arms would not have a part to play, but that the mass movement as opposed to the guerrilla forces must be the central actor in a revolutionary movement. Between 1980 and 1986, Chávez and Bravo met regularly. As a tutor at the Military Academy in Caracas, Chávez's influence over his young charges was growing; he was charming, eloquent, and much like them. And perhaps more importantly he had discovered a language of revolution rooted in Venezuelan experience. So too had Bravo, though there was a significant difference between the way in which the two men saw Bolívar. For Bravo, the Liberator was an inspiration, a symbolic figure whose history could drive forward a popular movement which could identify with his dedication and heroism. For Chávez, Bolívar was a successful soldier and, together with Robinson and Ezequiel Zamora, a guide and mentor. More profoundly, as time went on, Chávez increasingly emphasised the continuity between Bolívar and the late-twentieth-century movement that took his name. And for reasons we shall return to, that had a very particular and powerful impact as the century drew to its end, reinvigorating the project for national liberation in the context of a neo-liberalism that increasingly eliminated national frontiers in pursuit of globalisation.

Within the MBR Bravo was a far from popular figure and Chávez had kept his meeting from his fellow conspirators throughout. In fact the guerrilla leader had warned Chávez to restrain his excessive optimism and his determination to bring large numbers into the conspiracy. Opening the gates in this way would certainly alert the intelligence authorities as to the young officer's activities, and Bravo knew all too well how quickly that can undermine a clandestine project. Chávez accepted his advice, albeit reluctantly, and they continued to meet regularly. At one of their meetings, Chávez encountered the woman who would become his constant companion for the next few years. Herma Marksmann was a history lecturer; her sister Cristina was living in Caracas with Elizabeth Sánchez, whose house served as a meeting point for Bravo and his comrades. She was in the process of moving from Ciudad Bolívar to Caracas, and stayed each week with Sánchez, who would occasionally ask her to stay in her room while a mysterious meeting took place downstairs. She began to suspect what kind of meetings they were and asked for an explanation. Soon afterwards she met one of the participants – Hugo Chávez. Chávez was certainly not shy about his conquests, but Herma was more than just another brief encounter. She was an intelligent, attractive and politically aware companion who joined his political group after long conversations. Chávez respected her, and they were also in love, and he was given to extravagant romantic gestures – although he had had her investigated before proceeding with the relationship![16] Their relationship was to last for nine years, and end in bitterness.

Two years later Marksman was present at the third 'congress' of the MBR, signficant because it was the moment when Francisco Arias Cárdenas joined the group. Chávez had been anxious for some time to recruit Arias, whom he knew from the Academy. He was an impressive soldier, aligned with Causa R, and he was from Zulia, the oil province whose capital was Maracaibo, which any future movement must be able to control. The meeting, however, was stormy. The argument in San Cristobal had been carefully arranged and the people attending prepared for a possible escape. Perhaps this new level of caution had to do with the fact that there were signs that Chávez's activities at the academy had been discovered, or at the very least suspected. His posting to Elorza in Apure province, near the Colombian border, suggested that he was being deliberately marginalised. It was a very remote area, but Chávez used the opportunity to build relationships with local communities through his sporting prowess and the collective activities he organised with them. The possibility of discovery certainly added a sense of urgency to the group's activities. Yet Chávez, not for the last time, escaped further sanctions; it may be that he was just extremely lucky, or perhaps there were those in the upper echelons of the military who were not entirely hostile to his activities.

The meeting was argumentative because the underlying tensions in the group came to the surface in the debate with Arias. When Chávez described the role of the military as part of a wider social movement, Arias reacted by suggesting that these ideas sounded more like Douglas Bravo's and that what they were organising was a military action with popular support – but it was the radical soldiers who would be the chief actors in this process.

Chávez himself insists that he had already grown distant from Bravo and rejected his ideas.

My meeting with Maneiro and, why not come out and say it, my certainty that Douglas Bravo's direction was not the right one, pushed me closer to the Causa R, especially because of its work with the popular movements, which was vital to my still developing vision of the combined civilian-military struggle. I was very clear on the role of the masses, which Douglas's group were not; on the other hand, in the Causa R I felt the presence of the masses.[17]

In fact Causa R were going through a crisis at the time; their base in Catia and the universities was weakening and they had suffered serious defeats by AD in their most important area of work – the working-class organisations of Guayana. It is also a little disingenuous to suggest Bravo was not clear on the role of the masses – he had written for many years, and particularly through the 1970s, on precisely this topic.[18] These comments to Marta Haernecker, made much later, are a sign of his deliberate distancing from Bravo after the attempted coup in February 1992, though it had certainly begun earlier as he turned his attention to Causa R.

3

From Insurrection to Election

The Caracazo

In December 1988 Carlos Andrés Pérez, of Acción Democrática (AD), was re-elected to the Venezuelan Presidency. Much has been made of his charisma and his capacity to elude responsibility for his actions. But there was nothing magical about his electoral success. Pérez had overseen the oil boom years known as Saudi Venezuela, contracting an enormous public debt to finance his extravagant spending plans. As the boom collapsed Pérez handed on the presidential sash to Luis Herrera Campins of Copei, the junior partner in the Punto Fijo arrangements. But Herrera's administration oversaw a deepening crisis, manifest in the banking crisis of 1983, and his successor Jaime Lusinchi (1984–89) of AD succeeded mainly in enraging the mass of ordinary Venezuelans with even harsher austerity measures pressed on him by the IMF. As the crisis slowly unfolded, popular discontent deepened and new organs of local protest and resistance began to emerge in response. A transport strike in the Andean city of Mérida late in 1988 had been savagely repressed.

> The emerging conflict, expressed in the sharpening of the 'politics of the street' was not the result of the activism of any of the parties of the left. The proof is the twelve 'pobladas' – massive spontaneous popular demonstrations by communities demanding their rights – that took place in the course of 1988, prefiguring the event that more than any other expressed the crisis of governability – the events of 27th/28th of February.[1]

Despite the fact that he also represented AD, which had imposed those measures, Pérez managed to build on his reputation as the man who had presided over the boom years, and raise expectations among the electorate. And he repeatedly promised during his campaign that he would reverse the crippling programme of cuts – he memorably called it 'una bomba que sólo mata gente' – a bomb that only kills people (the Star Wars bomb announced by US President Ronald Reagan did just that – leaving buildings intact!). Yet it took only a matter of weeks for the emptiness of his undertakings to be exposed, with the 'gran viraje', the about-turn with which CAP abandoned all his electoral promises and bent the knee to the IMF. Within days he appeared on television to announce the adoption of a series of emergency austerity measures whose burden would fall mainly on Venezuela's poor, but also on significant sections of the middle class. On 25 February Pérez announced that petrol prices would rise; the effects would be felt, of course, across the whole economy. More importantly it was a basic assumption of every Venezuelan that cheap petrol was a right, given that Venezuela was a major oil-producing nation. Two days later, the local buses that brought people into the city from the hillside barrios told their passengers when they tried to board them that the fares had gone up. It was the final straw. In Guarenas, a poor suburb, a woman passenger refused to pay the increased fare. The driver (like most bus drivers he was an individual owner) tried to remove her. The other passengers erupted, overturning the bus and setting fire to it. The fires spread as rapidly as the news. Caracas exploded in rage and frustration – it was the morning of 27 February 1989, a date as emblematic in the social history of Venezuela as it was a milestone in the history of Hugo Chávez and the movement that would carry him to the presidency, and beyond.

The Caracazo is often described as a spontaneous outburst of popular rage, as such insurrectionary risings usually are – they are 'riots' or 'explosions', characterised by their lack of a common objective, their inchoate violence, their component of vengeance. This is rarely a true or complete reflection of such events. The anger of whole communities is cumulative and continuous; it has a history embedded in a popular memory. Ideally, in the history of the left at least, that popular memory has its incarnation in one or several political parties. But in reality political organisations rarely reflect the consciousness or experience of these often disenfranchised groups in society who have little or no means of speaking truth to power. Yet that popular memory exists in every community, manifested through a symbolic vocabulary and a shared imaginary expressed in music, urban myth and legend, festivals and ritual, secret languages, and often in forms of popular religion. These are usually very localised and transmitted through a language of word and gesture that can be impenetrable to the wider world – a form of protection against repression and incorporation. 'The protest quickly turned into a major social upheaval with barricades, road closures and looting spreading across the country. Passing food trucks were detained by protestors, their cargo unloaded and their vehicles parked across the highway.'[2]

The immediate reaction of the government was slow. On the first day of the Caracazo only the police were in evidence, and in some areas – the San José barrio for example – they were seen to impose some order on the looting in collusion with the rioters. But by that evening the government of Carlos Andrés Pérez had announced a curfew. Since the National Guard had refused to go into the barrios, probably out of fear rather than solidarity, the army was sent in to enforce the curfew. The masses, however, had taken the streets of towns and cities across Venezuela. The troops moved into the high rise districts of the Pérez Jiménez era, in Caracas, and into the hills, 'shooting anything that moved', as Richard Gott put it. The official figure of 350 dead on that first day was certainly an underestimate, at least according to the victims of this ferocious repression. By the end of the following day the estimates rose to 3,000 dead and thousands wounded. The persistent rumour was that they were buried in unmarked graves. On 3 March the iconic 23 de Enero barrio was surrounded and attacked by the army with consequences that are still uncounted, though the likelihood is that it raised the total to 5,000. Repression on this level has other objectives, beyond killing identifiable leaders and frightening the population into returning to their homes. Its purpose was to create a climate of fear, to inflict a long term defeat and wherever possible to erase these events from the collective memory.[3]

A 'social protest' of course is very different from a riot. While the press abounds with scare stories and pictures of people dragging sides of beef, fridges and consumer goods from smashed up supermarkets, the meaning of these actions is lost. They *are* acts of protest, and at some level acts of redistribution; they are also invariably acts of retaliation, not for any specific offence but for the offence of inequality and mal-distribution of wealth, the vengeance of the poor. The question is whether this response is a challenge to power, the embryo of another form of society, however brief its existence. For Roland Denis, a well respected radical activist of many years standing, the insurrection was a political expression.

> An extraordinary rebellion that, although its protagonists were the least organised and most marginalised sectors of society, left in its wake a legacy of autonomy and confrontation with the political rationality of parties and with the obedience to the prevailing bourgeois republican order which without a doubt will take us far beyond the spirit of past insurgencies.[4]

The debate around the character and significance of the Caracazo continued and still continues within and on the margins of Chavismo. There is broad agreement, however, that the Bolivarian revolution in one sense or another began in February 1989. What that sense is is vigorously disputed. At one level the riots can be seen as manifestations of rage and despair, evidence of the reality of a spurious democracy which acted on behalf of the interests of a corrupt and self-serving minority against those of the majority. And the vicious repression of the Caracazo was testimony to the violence inherent in a bourgeois democracy, unmasking the myth of Venezuela's unique stability. That is incontestable. The argument centres on the character of the popular response, and in particular on the extent to which it represented the beginning of the end of the domination of Venezuelan politics by the *puntofijista* party machines.

In the Aftermath

Chávez was now back in Caracas and the MBR-200 was drawing in new conspirators. But it remained just that – a military conspiracy, though Chávez was still pursuing civilian political contacts. He was distancing himself more and more from Douglas Bravo, while developing his contacts with Causa R. Yet Causa R's strength was still in Ciudad Guyana and the industrial plants of Bolívar state; its early base of support in the Central University of Venezuela in Caracas and the Catia district had been significantly weakened. Whatever his opinion of Douglas Bravo, the old guerrilla leader was almost certainly more closely in touch with grassroots activism than any of the other civilian contacts on whom Chávez relied. And the reality was that, although it had a general perception of the rising discontents across the country, MBR-200 was completely unprepared for the Caracazo. Even the notorious state security service, Disip, had seemed unaware of the potential explosion to come. This was not because the signs were not there, but rather that Disip did not pay very much attention to events inside the barrios but was concentrating on the activities of left wing *parties*. Many of the MBR conspirators were forced to participate in the appalling repression that followed – and one of the original group, Felipe Acosta Carles, was killed during those February days. Given his position Chávez himself was fortunate not to have been called to join the repressive operation.

As chance would have it, Chávez was ill with a serious infection and confined to bed, and watched the unfolding events on television. It is easy to imagine how horrified he must have been, and also how urgent he felt it to be to address the problem that the Caracazo had revealed for the MBR-200 itself. In the earlier vehement discussions with Arias Cárdenas, Arias had emphasised his conviction that the military rebels should organise separately. He had voiced his suspicions of joint activities with civilian organisations, partly because of the security risks he saw that as representing, and partly because he firmly believed that the challenge to the state had to be led by a disciplined, military cadre. At this critical stage, it seemed clear that these were the ideas that prevailed inside the MBR-200. As a result, although there had been discussions of how they should respond in the event of a popular uprising, the discussion had not been taken further.

Richard Gott argues that the consequence of this terrible state violence was a long term political apathy.[5] Yet there is significant evidence to the contrary. It is true that the activities of political parties on the ground were seriously affected. In the barrios and communities autonomous, grassroots organising continued in many areas, sometimes inspired by liberation theology. There is also the evidence of the elections of December 1989, when the candidate of Causa R, Andrés Velásquez, was elected to the governorship of Bolívar state (and re-elected four years later for a second term). The Movement Toward Socialism (MAS), led by ex-guerrilla leader Teodoro Petkoff, also dramatically increased its vote in the municipal elections of that year and began to work with Acción Democrática within the trade unions. In the mid-1990s, Petkoff would accept a post as Economics Minister with direct responsibility for applying IMF-ordered austerity measures. On the walls of the barrios, graffiti asserted the deepening anger of the people.

For Hugo Chávez and his group, the Caracazo had caused serious internal problems. 'We began to accelerate our organising, our search for civilian contacts and popular movements, to think about ideology and above all, about strategy; how to transcend one situation and find a transition to a better one.'[6]

The formulation is odd, since the group already had a Bolivarian ideology, but the Caracazo had probably revealed its limitations. It had also created a greater sense of urgency as the military conspirators came face to face with the tasks they could still be asked to fulfil by a state which they had agreed was corrupt and thoroughly undemocratic. Richard Gott quotes Arias Cárdenas' anguish and the instructions he gave to those under his command: 'The people who live here are like us, they are our people, our brothers (and sisters); that means that no-one must fire without authorization, no-one must shoot unless we are attacked.'[7]

Other soldiers, hearing rumours about MBR-200, began to approach Chávez. The army command were hearing the same rumours, and summoned Chávez and others to a hearing. Chávez himself says that he was in custody in December, when Velásquez won the Bolívar gubernatorial election. In the days following he appeared before the tribunal to answer the accusation that he was part of a plot to murder the President. Curiously, the authorities took no action – and Chávez was allowed to attend the Simón Bolívar

University to study for a Masters degree in political science. It is a curious facet of Chávez's early career that he managed repeatedly to avoid sanctions for his organising activities. He clearly enjoyed the protection of some high-ranking officers who were not sympathetic to the corrupt bureaucratic elite ruling the country.

The Caracazo raised again the question of the relationship between the military rebels and other social forces. In its aftermath Chávez renewed some of the earlier contacts he had had with the 'civilian' left. And MBR-200 was not the only group at work within the armed forces. William Izarra's R-83, now renamed ARMA (The Revolutionary Alliance of Serving Officers), was active and had maintained closer contacts with the revolutionary left; and there were also secret cells at work in the Navy. Izarra's name does not arise in Chávez's conversations with Marta Haernecker, however, although he would play a key role in the first Chavista government. Chávez did renew his contact with Douglas Bravo after the February events. The two men met again, together with others, including some radical priests, in Caracas. In Bravo's view, the Caracazo had 'created the conditions for a reactivation of the civic-military-religious alliance'.[8] For Bravo, it represented the re-emergence of the forces that had overthrown the government of Pérez Jiménez in 1958, and it posed the same key political questions – the necessity of coordination between revolutionaries within the military and the civilian movement, and the creation of new forms of organisation that could reflect that relationship and operate democratically. In 1958 it had been the temptations of access to state power that had largely undermined the movement. And it would prove once again to be seductive enough to tempt key figures on the left, like Petkoff. But while Bravo located the leadership of the movement firmly in the civilian organisations, Chávez saw that role as belonging to the military rebels. That had been the position of Arias Cárdenas, for example.

On the other hand, the Caracazo had shown that it would be imperative to coordinate the two. That was one reason why Chávez was also reactivating his relationship with Causa R and meeting with its new leader, Pablo Medina. The problem was the relationship between the MBR and the mass movement. Causa R's continuing support in the industrial areas in Bolívar state seemed to offer Chávez the opportunity to put in place his idea for 'dignity battalions' (a concept first developed by Torrijos in Panama) – groups of armed civilians who might be ready to act in support of the military. Yet it was very clear that the leadership of them would remain with the military. That was not what Bravo was arguing for; Medina, for his part, nervously accepted the idea, but there was little progress in organising the battalions.

The MBR was now actively planning a coup, and there appeared to be no disagreement within the group about that objective. They had no plan or strategy, however, for what would happen after the seizure of power. Kléber Martínez Rojas, an engineer and a long standing member of Bravo's PRV, was now called out of retirement and charged with drawing up a manifesto; it would later form the basis of the Movement of the Fifth Republic (MVR). Kléber argued for a Bolivarianism rooted in the mass movements but distanced from the old parties.[9]

It had been agreed within the MBR-200 that when both Arias and Chávez became eligible for a command, in 1990, they would be in a position to organise the coup. The first action plan had identified December 1991 as the moment when the right conditions existed. Chávez had command of a tank regiment, and Urdaneta and Arias had their own commands in Maracay and Maracaibo respectively. In the event the December plan was aborted after the plans were leaked. More importantly, it had also become clear that Chávez envisaged a military action with the *support*, but not the active participation of the mass movement. Their disagreement on this issue ended the collaboration between Bravo and Chávez for the second time. Pablo Medina, for his part, withdrew his support at the last minute – and in doing so removed any possibility of the involvement of the 'dignity battalions' of workers. He would later say that Chávez was a 'sponge', absorbing ideas from everywhere.

There were other setbacks for Chávez too. Having completed his commander's course he was assigned to an administrative post in Cumaná, in the east of the country, rather than the command he expected. It was, he said, 'a slap in the face'.[10] But a few weeks later the command of a parachute battalion in Maracay fell vacant, and it was given to Chávez by the then Minister of Defence, Ochoa. The office of military intelligence was aware of Chávez's conspiratorial activities, yet its reaction was to send him for psychiatric evaluation. Once again, Chávez had evaded more serious sanctions. He now had an important and influential command, but the Caracazo had impacted on the whole of the army. In fact towards the end of December 1991 a group of captains threatened to launch their own coup (probably under the influence of Bandera Roja) unless the MBR moved. Chávez explains:'I had to threaten some of the captains that I'd tie them to a tree if they tried anything, and I had to go to Caracas and get into Miraflores and speak to the soldiers there and tell our people that unless they received a written order signed by me, with a password, nothing was happening'.[11]

The tension within the armed forces was rising, and there were rumours circulating that Chávez had done a deal with the Defence Ministry. It appeared that details of the December coup had possibly been leaked, inadvertently, by Kleber; this added to the internal strains within the MBR. Urdaneta had already expressed unease at Chávez's contacts with Bravo as well as his objections to what he felt was Chávez's tendency to make plans without consulting the other members of the group. As 1992 began, further increases in transport and telephone charges were announced by an ever more unpopular Pérez, and there were renewed protests in the barrios and demonstrations by teachers and university students. The trade unions were demanding a 50 per cent wage increase; the response was a 35 per cent increase – for the military only! It was, Chávez felt, the last chance to launch their action. The decision was taken to launch the coup when Pérez returned from a visit to Switzerland, where he had joined the representatives of global capital at the World Economic Forum. That day proved to be 4 February 1992.

Por Ahora – For Now

In fact Pérez landed in Maiquetia airport at 10 p.m. on 3 February. Unsually, he was met by Defence Minister Ochoa, who informed him of the rumours of an imminent coup. At about the same time, in Maracay (about an hour away from Caracas), Chávez mobilised the 460 members of his parachute regiment, and crowded them on to buses he had hired ostensibly for a military exercise in Cojedes province. In fact only a small group was aware of Plan Zamora, the coming military coup. Just before midnight Pérez was woken with news that the Zulia garrison had risen under Arias Cárdenas. Within minutes Pérez arrived at the Miraflores presidential palace in Caracas; at almost the same time, Chávez arrived in Caracas and entered the Museum of Military History which, symbolically, was to be his headquarters. Elsewhere in the city the coup supporters moved into action – the airbase of La Carlota was taken and held after a brief shootout, while two tank captains had been dispatched to Miraflores where they were driving their clumsy vehicles up the central entrance stairway. Pérez meanwhile had escaped from the palace and made his way to Channel 4 TV whose proprietor, Cisneros, was one of Venezuela's wealthiest and most powerful capitalists. When Chávez turned to the state channel on the television at the museum, he was expecting to see a broadcast of his pre-recorded video in which he explained why the coup had been launched. The studios had been occupied by rebel troops, but they had not been able to transmit the video. Instead, at around 1 a.m., what he saw was a dishevelled Carlos Andrés Pérez denouncing their action as an assault on democracy. The attempt to take Miraflores had failed and Pérez remained free. And while La Carlota and the Maracaibo garrison were under the control of rebel troops, and fighting was continuing in Maracay, the reality just four hours after its launch was that Operation Zamora had failed. Its central objective, the capture of Pérez, was never a real possibility. And as one final humiliation, Fidel Castro had sent Pérez a telegram congratulating him on surviving the coup![12]

With the Military Museum surrounded and two F-16s threateningly overflying it, Chávez informed the two envoys sent by Defence Minister Ochoa that he was ready to surrender. He was subsequently accused of cowardice, but he retorted that since it was obvious that they had lost his concern was to avoid futile bloodshed. And that seems consistent. Yet the rebellions elsewhere in the country had not ended, and Ochoa argued for giving Chávez a minute on television to call on his people to surrender too. It would prove to be a mistake of enormous proportions, especially since the decision was to allow him to broadcast live rather than record (and later edit) his speech. His appearance lasted one minute and consisted of less than 200 words; he acknowledged the failure of the coup, called on his comrades to lay down their arms and took public responsibility for the action.

'Comrades, unfortunately for now [*por ahora*] we have not achieved our objectives here in the capital. That is, here in Caracas, we have failed to take power ... .'

Two words, apparently unrehearsed, turned defeat into a long term victory.

Over time, the events of 4 February have come to be seen as the beginning of the epic of Chavismo, despite the fact that by any criterion, it was a failure. It is no exaggeration that the two words, *por ahora*, turned Chávez into a popular hero; here was a military officer who took responsibility for his actions, and promised to repeat them. When the words began to appear on walls around the city, they required no explanation.

Why had the coup failed? According to Douglas Bravo, it was Chávez's reluctance to involve the people directly that prevented its chances of success.[13] Roland Denis takes a similar view, noting that the civic–military alliance was in its infancy and as yet unorganised. Further, both at the time and more emphatically later, it was represented within a narrative of conspiratorial actions secretly prepared and executed by a small group. This of course was true, but its resonances were complex and ambivalent. As Denis puts it:

Despite the military failure of the rebel operation, the subversive self-confidence of people increased dramatically. The support for the coup on the street became immediately obvious ... and it strengthened the feeling of opposition to the system, gave an enormous boost to civil resistance and undoubtedly added credibility to the political ideas that were beginning to circulate without the aid of television but transmitted by word of mouth and a great deal of paper.[14]

This support came above all because these were young officers from poor backgrounds, men like Chávez, men like themselves. And their discourse was not the well-worn reassurances about democracy, but the language of liberty, justice nationhood and the people. Chávez,

Figure 4.1 Chávez in prison (© Luis Noguera)

unlike any other politician within living memory, had taken public responsibility for his actions. At the critical moment, he had taken a giant step towards winning the leadership, at the symbolic level at least, of the still diverse, sometimes chaotic universe of daily struggle of all poor Venezuelans. It was not yet a movement, since it had found no form of common organisation; but it was a rainbow spectrum of resistance – a many-headed hydra – and it was in a rebellious mood.

Chávez was now transferred to the San Carlos prison where so many revolutionaries and resisters had been brutally tortured under earlier AD governments.[15] A military tribunal set up by the Defence Minister to investigate the causes of the coup concluded that it had to do with specific internal conditions and discontents within the armed forces, rather than being a reflection of a divided and unequal society and of popular anger at the corruption, bureaucracy and ineptitude characteristic of previous governments.

For many Venezuelans, the inhabitants of the barrios, the working class suffering savage cuts in wages and living standards, the small peasant farmers facing the arbitrary justice of the landowners and their hired thugs, this was what Hugo Chávez refracted and symbolised. His cell at San Carlos must have felt like a railway station at times, with its constant stream of visitors which the prison authorities did little to stop. Many were ordinary people who had come to meet this curious figure who seemed so much less alien to them than previous generations of politicians. Of course, he was not a politician, but something else. Chávez reports the visit of an army chaplain who presented him with a Bible (Chávez was always deeply religious) and whispered in his ear, 'You are a hero'. Herma Marksman was deeply uneasy about Chávez's response to his new celebrity status – indeed, according to her, their relationship began to fail at that moment.[16] 'Hugo suddenly thinks he's Rock Hudson, signing autographs for his fans', she said, with obvious bitterness. There were female visitors who would gladly have replaced her, among them, so it is rumoured, the journalist Laura Sánchez who interviewed him on a number of occasions. The left sought him out and he became an object of admiration for intellectuals and artists. More importantly he was visited by other MBR-200 members and messengers, because others were planning a second attempt at a military coup. This second group was led by Admiral Hernán Gruber and Francisco Visconti from the air force. Chávez was later moved to Yare prison, two hours drive from Caracas, but he continued to build his networks and connections and to communicate with the new plotters with his brother Argenis acting as go-between. One plan had been to assassinate Pérez on 5 July; it did not happen, but the group of soldiers in Yare called themselves the 5 July group nonetheless. Gruber and Visconti began planning their coup in earnest in August. Gruber in particular was deeply angered by the corruption within the army and it had become obvious by August that the high command would not or could not address the problem. And at the same time, the echoes of the February coup could still be heard in the poor districts and working-class areas, where the protests continued, led often by portraits of Chávez and the shouting of his name. In the Carnival processions that year, there were a number of kids dressed as Chávez.

On 27 November, the second coup was launched, this time with more violence. Miraflores was bombed, La Carlota airbase was seized again and a television station was taken. Unfortunately, or ironically, the video that Gruber had prepared to explain their actions was somehow switched. That was hardly designed to inspire the people whose support he had intended to seek! This time a popular rising was anticipated, but nothing had been done to organise it, though a plan for a new government had been elaborated, with names attached. Although there were armed confrontations in the street, and more deaths than in February, the coup lasted very little longer than in February. It left 171 dead, 95 injured and 1,340 people were detained. Chávez now found himself with some new companions in Yare.

Whatever his denials, Chávez himself was clearly affected and flattered by his new heroic status. But he was not simply the passive object of the adoration of others. He was actively promoting himself as a sort of reincarnation of Bolívar, the person charged with continuing his project. Marksman felt that he was falling into a kind of Messianic fervour which this identification with Bolívar exemplified. And more profoundly, there was in this affirmation of continuity a political perception. The Caracazo and the subsequent years had brought the logic of collective action and participation to the forefront; the heroic myth created a different logic of change, a logic of heroic leaders acting *on behalf of* the community. Who were to be the active subjects of the future revolution? The working class, the mass social movements or a small group of heroic leaders? The tension between these two political visions, and their strategic consequences, would persist in the Bolivarian movement from then on, and into the present. And there was, in some sense, an eerie echo here of the debate that had increasingly absorbed Bolívar's own later years. Reflecting back on these events 20 years later, the documentary called *La Quijotada* (2013), broadcast by the television channel that Chávez had established in 2005, Telesur,[17] represented the popular protests as responses to orders from Chávez, rather than the self-organised actions of an enraged and resisting community.

And they had every reason to resist. Finance Minister Miguel Rodríguez's economic measures were biting hard. After the Caracazo, and the repression that followed the announcement of increases in the price of petrol, electricity and telephones, new measures were added. By 1991 the top tenth of the population was earning 24 times the income of the lowest tenth (doubling the figure for 1984).[18] In Venezuela, as elsewhere in Latin America, neo-liberalism brought increased inequality, impoverishment on a huge scale, and the deepening dependence of national states on the international financial agencies. The beneficiaries were those who acted as their agents. By 1998 per capita income in Venezuela was 8 per cent less than in 1970, the income of workers was reduced by half and the profits of capital rose by 15 per cent in the same period. Between 1984 and 1991, poverty levels in the country doubled (from 36 per cent to 68 per cent of the population).

'These crisis-like conditions became permanent features of society. We are dealing here not with the exclusion of a minority categorised as "marginal" in relation to society as a whole but with the living conditions and cultural reproduction of the great majority of the population.'[19]

And yet they lived in a political system in which they felt, correctly, that they were not represented in any way. Given the lack of any clear political alternative in the mid-1990s, it was correct for Chávez to call for abstention from voting in the 1993 presidential elections. In fact they were a success for the legal left, principally MAS and Causa R. Carlos Andrés Pérez's luck finally ran out as his corrupt activities were exposed; he was facing trial for them as the election approached. The veteran Rafael Caldera assumed he would be the COPEI candidate, but when he was squeezed out, he formed an electoral alliance (*Convergencia*) with MAS and won the presidency with 30 per cent of the vote. Abstention reached 40 per cent, but the major surprise was the 22 per cent won by Andrés Velásquez of Causa R (though it was widely believed his vote had been much higher in reality). Similarly, direct voting for state governors opened some political space for those parties outside the *puntofijista* arrangement. In fact, Causa R's huge advance in the polls provoked an internal crisis which would eventually lead to its division; finding itself unexpectedly close to power, it entered into alliances with the old parties, together with MAS, discrediting itself among those who had hoped that perhaps these two organisations, with their history, might resist the blandishments and temptations of power. They did not.

Caldera, for his part, very soon disappointed those who might have had expectations of him. His government immediately introduced measures, called the *Agenda Venezuela*, which involved privatisation, the elimination of price and currency controls, and the end of the social security system. The bitter irony was that the minister in charge of introducing these measures was Teodoro Petkoff, the ex-guerrilla who led MAS. The regional elections of 1995 confirmed the disillusionment of voters with what might have seemed like an alternative. They were as locked in to the old corrupt system of patronage and manipulation as AD and COPEI, though the split in Causa R left one section with some credibility after they broke with a manifestly power-hungry Velásquez. They would later form a different party, PPT (Patria para Todos) in 1997 and join Chávez, incidentally providing him with some of his most respected and experienced collaborators.

Caldera released Chávez in March 1994, as evidence of his conciliatory intentions. Chávez's luck, it seemed, was still holding. He seemed a different person from the conspirator of the previous decade. He was now a public figure whose name and image were ubiquitous. And the symbolism of Bolívar, whose image and words accompanied him everywhere, served this transformation. He had appropriated from the old elite the image that best represented the desire for national sovereignty and had expanded it to embrace a vigorous and combative anti-imperialism. In the era of globalisation that could not fail to mobilise the majority of Venezuelans. And it was not only the poor and the working class who gravitated towards him. Despite an enduring unease with the military (people still remembered Pérez Jiménez) part of the middle classes were drawn towards him too. They had suffered dramatically, particularly in the banking crisis of 1993, and neither were they exempt from the impact of privatisation and price increases. They will also have noted how the single source of Venezuelan's wealth, the oil that was responsible for the boom of the 1970s, was now administered by a national oil corporation, Pdvsa, which had put itself beyond state control, making independent agreements with foreign, mainly United States, interests, over-producing and thus undermining OPEC and operating under its director Luis Giusti[20] like any other multinational corporation. Chávez's critique of puntofijismo, his attack on corruption, and his promise of a Venezuela that was authentically democratic thus had a growing appeal.

Out of prison, Chávez set himself a demanding pace. He moved restlessly and constantly around the country, speaking, shaking hands, meeting the people. He stayed with friends, ate where he could, and exhibited that legendary energy and loquacity which would make him such a visible figure on the world stage when he occupied the presidency. His line on elections was pithy, and cleverly used his famous quip of 1992, 'Por ahora, por ninguno' – For now (vote) for no-one. After the notoriety of 1992, and his high visibility after February, Chávez was given less prominence in the media; but the barrios had no need for the newspapers to remind them of his existence. He appeared and reappeared in public spaces around the country, travelling tirelessly, speaking until he was hoarse however small or large his audience. He and Nancy had recently divorced amicably and while he kept in touch with his children, whom he clearly adored, it was as often as not a telephone call explaining why he could not be with them. But the divorce freed him for the 24-hour existence of an insomniac with a mission. And wherever he went, he was always receiving visitors. In those days the photographs show a man often dressed in the traditional white suit of the llanos, the *liqui-liqui*, rather than a uniform. It was not just a sartorial choice, it was a political decision to bridge the distance from the people that a uniform creates.

Roland Denis reports how, at a meeting in Catia where he was wearing a uniform, he removed his pistol and set it on the floor. It was a piece of theatre, a metaphorical declaration that he was like his listeners. 'In those first years, 1994 to 1995, we hadn't ruled out the possibility of reverting to the armed struggle, but we wanted to evaluate the possibility in terms of our real forces, and we concluded that we didn't have those forces.'[21]

In fact the social movements were passing through a period of reversal. It was as if, in the wake of the excitement of 1992, the actions of the old left in imposing austerity programmes had demoralised and disappointed many people. At the same time, there was an active process of political discussion going on, and a slow rebuilding of the political spaces outside the institutions. And Chávez's proposals were certainly part of that rebuilding, because it seemed that the recognition of the limited possibilities of MBR-200 within the army had led him to try to rebuild the civic part of the civic–military alliance and renew his contacts with the organised left. Certainly he was in conversation with people like Alí Rodríguez Araque, who would become his Oil Minister and Aristóbulo Istúriz, the popular teachers leader who was elected Mayor of Caracas in 1992. Both belonged to the faction of Causa R that later became Patria Para Todos, and entered into the electoral alliance with Chávez. He was also actively working on a plan for government. Jorge Giordani, an economist and a member of MAS, spent a great deal of time with him; first in prison, where he was supervising his master's thesis and later wherever he happened to be in his ceaseless travels. Kleber worked with him on the issue of institutional reform. And, as Chávez affirms, there were long discussions on the subject of a Constituent Assembly. All of these pointed to a programme of government, of course, but not the ready made replacement leadership that Gruber had prepared before 29 November with no consultation with the wider movement. Chávez's travels, and his renewed contacts with the left, were a kind of research trip, a plebiscite in practice; between 1996 and 1997, Chávez reports, they conducted a more formal survey asking the very specific question – would you vote for Chávez?

The issue of the Constituent Assembly will arise a little later, but what was clear by then was that the MBR-200, although still an essentially military grouping, was beginning to see itself as a political organisation, an expression of the civic–military alliance. This reflected several changes. Chávez had discharged himself from the army after 4 February; those MBR members who had remained were under surveillance and very restricted in what they could do. But that was circumstantial. The more important point was that Chávez was beginning to see himself as a political leader and a potential president – hence the survey question. It began to be possible now to speak of *chavismo* as a movement, but it was significant that the movement bore the name of its leader rather than any statement of its political objectives. It was true of course that as the material situation of most Venezuelans worsened, as extreme poverty became visible on the streets, and as the moral and political collapse of the old political system continued, Chávez came to represent and embody a general rejection of both neo-liberalism and puntofijismo. And he was drawing around him a wide range of people who could claim to share that vision of the national reality. The existing left parties split over the question of whether Chávez could successfully mount a challenge and forge a new alliance of the military, the social movements, and sections of the political establishment. Causa R's internal crisis led to a split and the PPT section moved into alliance with him. The wily political operator, Luis Miquilena, one of history's great survivors, brought to the alliance long experience on the communist left and in the trade unions. Giordani came from a MAS that had chosen to support Chávez despite the immovable refusal of Teodoro Petkoff, the party leader, to agree. PPT brought the Medina wing of Causa R. and other independents threw their weight behind his candidacy, like Pedro Duno, the influential and respected philosopher. Another who had joined him was William Izarra, the revolutionary organiser of the ARMA group within the armed forces. When he joined the MBR, in 1996, his impression was that it was a revolutionary perspective that prevailed in Chávez's circle, that its objective was the seizure of power, and the overthrow of the bourgeois state – though there was considerable debate as to whether this meant an armed coup or another kind of movement.

In fact, Chávez had become committed to the electoral strategy. The MBR Congress that met early in 1997 was a tense and argumentative affair, and the majority of MBR's members (between 2,000 and 3,000 at the time) were opposed to Chávez's proposal to participate in the forthcoming election. For many of them, it seemed like a betrayal of the fundamental principle of the organisation – its unrelenting hostility to the existing political system and its refusal to participate in its corrupt and clientilistic methods. In fact, Chávez found himself – very unusually – in a minority at the Congress. Names that would later become familiar, like Nicolás Maduro and Freddy Bernal (later Mayor of Caracas), rejected his arguments. Chávez then threatened to resign. Maduro and others understood that his role was so critical that the group could not survive without him, and they then worked to support him,[22] though they certainly did not anticipate at that stage that he would win the presidency. The Movement of the Fifth Republic (MVR) was then established as the political party whose candidate Chávez would be.

The tensions within the MBR were not resolved by that decision, however; there were probably three basic strategic visions at play within the organisation and, as will emerge later, the future of Chavismo would continue to be debated between them well into the twenty-first century. The origins of the MBR shaped the insurrection-ary, armed struggle current that informed its early years. A military coup is a clandestine matter, whose success depends on discipline and a structure of command. The 4 February attempted coup was not collectively decided; decisions were made by a small group and the order of march delivered to the bulk of participants only at the last minute – for obvious reasons, perhaps, to do with security. The method, as has been argued and debated across the Latin American left since the Cuban Revolution, did not lend itself to democratic participation. The second position derived from the political experience of mass mobilisation in Venezuela. The support for Chávez through the 1990s had come from a wide range of organisations that developed essentially as forms of defence in the face of neo-liberalism. They mobilised around protests, demonstrations, forms of community organisation, cooperatives, cultural groups, alternative media and education collectives – together they represented the resistance which had accepted Chávez precisely because he had come from *outside* the discredited political system. If the political logic of a command structure led towards forms of leadership, the logic of the popular resistance (and not just in the barrios but across a much wider spectrum)[23] pointed in the direction of a participatory democracy as an alternative to a representative, parliamentary form. How that could express itself was the subject of energetic debate across the movement through the mid-1990s. The third position, now reluctantly agreed, was some form of electoral democracy, albeit one which was not dominated by political parties (Chávez was adamant about that at this stage), was immune to patronage and clientilism, which was transparent and in which representatives were subject to recall. The ambiguity at its heart, of course, was that it seemed to presume that the state could be transformed from within and over time – a *process*, which was very different from a revolutionary seizure of the state, by whatever means. And the issue would not be resolved by the election of Chávez to the presidency.

The ambivalence of many in the MBR confirmed once again the two contradictory impulses at work within the movement. On the one hand, the drive to create the possibility of a radical democracy born out of the organs of mass struggle; on the other, the election of an alternative government, which would be different from all the previous ones. But the sole guarantee of that would be Chávez himself. Luis Miquilena was a key factor in changing Chávez's mind; significantly, he now appeared in a suit and tie – dress was always a signal to be carefully read where Chávez was concerned.[24]

Early polls showed Chávez with a low level of support as compared to his opponent, the very tall, very white mayor of the elegant Chacao district of Caracas, and ex-Miss Venezuela, Irene Sáez, who was supported by Petkoff and Andrés Velásquez among others; she openly advocated neo-liberal solutions. Yet Chávez's own polls had shown that 57 per cent of those consulted would vote for him for president. As it turned out, his polls were uncannily accurate.

4

Episodes in the Class War

Constituting the Future

The Venezuela that Hugo Chávez inherited from Rafael Caldera was in deep crisis. Like Caldera's predecessor and mirror image in the Venezuelan political system, Carlos Andrés Pérez, he had promised on the campaign trial to resist them and promptly imposed the austerity measures imposed by the IMF once elected. His chief executioner was until recently a man of the left, Teodoro Petkoff. Between them they brought an already ailing Venezuelan economy to its knees. A devaluation in 1993 repeated the one ten years earlier, with even more dramatic effects – hitting particularly the middle classes. The privatisations and price increases hit the poorer sections disproportionately, many of them figuring among the 25 per cent of Venezuelans living in extreme poverty on the eve of the election. The number living below acceptable living standards in the country, according to the United Nations, ranged between 65 and 70 per cent. The telephone company (Cantv), the steel manufacturer (Sidor) and the national airline (Viasa) were all sold to private interests, together with 'a long list of financial institutions, sugar mills, naval shipyards and companies in the construction sector'.[1]

In the decade since the Caracazo, the situation in the country had grown dramatically worse. That in itself would be sufficient explanation for the electoral victory of Hugo Chávez, the only candidate who could claim to be untainted by involvement in the political system that produced this economic and social disaster. And it is important to remember that while the very poorest were the most affected, they were not the only ones exposed to the ill effects of what was still euphemistically called at the time 'structural adjustment'. The 56 per cent who supported him certainly included a significant section of the middle class too, of professionals, left activists, university lecturers and students, teachers, nurses and working class people outside the privileged areas of state employment who suffered badly with the devaluation and the price inflation that followed. And equally, while abstention levels have historically been low in Venezuela (but not as low as they would be under Chávez) they would have included significant numbers of people in the barrios and remote rural regions who later voted consistently for him. And the final blow was the lacklustre candidates put up against him.

Of course lacklustre candidates had won the presidency on many occasions in the past – but always with the solid support and vote-rigging capacity of the *puntofijista* parties, as well as the enthusiastic backing of the powerful economic interests whom they so faithfully served, both internal and external, and the mass media that they owned. Hugo Chávez had none of these instruments at his disposal. His political machine, if it can be called that, was the local support networks that the MBR had begun to build in the wake of its decision to move towards becoming a political organisation, which were enthusiastic but small in number. And there were also the organisations that had joined him in the MVR and the Polo Patriótico electoral alliance. Each of them brought votes and some activists, located across the social spectrum. What they did not possess were the levels of media coverage that Chávez's opponents enjoyed. At other times, that might have been enough, together with the *puntofijista* machine, to guarantee sufficient votes to even the dullest candidate.

But that machine was no longer functioning, its inner workings exposed for all to see and its deterioration beyond denial. And in fact he had the support of the country's leading media baron, Cisneros, and of the country's leading newspaper, *El Nacional*.

These were the circumstances in which Hugo Chávez, a man loathed by the bourgeoisie and their friends for the colour of his skin, the manner of his speech, and his patent and ostentatious disrespect for the elite and their rituals, presented himself to the electorate in December 1998. Yet these were the very characteristics that endeared him to the wider movement, to the people in the barrios, the trade unionists, the left organisations, the precariously balanced lower-middle classes, who gave him their vote. And he was, without doubt, incredibly skilled in deploying them to the greatest advantage. He was, as everyone agrees, a brilliant communicator with a charisma that everyone who has encountered him comments on. He looked and sounded like someone who understood the lives of the people he was speaking to. His language, his Bolivarian discourse, appealed to a shared imaginary and identified shared enemies – the crooked *puntofijista* politicians, the utterly corrupt Carlos Andrés Pérez, the colonels and generals who did the bidding of the politicians – and who had recently launched another wave of political persecution – and the United States, with its hands on Venezuela's throat. Chávez presented himself in a single historical line from Bolívar and Rodríguez through Zamora, all of whom fought and were prepared to suffer for an ideal of national independence. The combination of dull opponents and the vibrant, cheerful, storytelling singing candidate of the people who took pride in his rude and disrespectful responses to the elite began to make victory seem possible. Throughout 1998 support committees began to be formed in barrios and communities, People's Assemblies gathered to discuss the future, land occupations increased, new educational centres were set up and the grassroots and community media began to flourish. On the other hand, familiar faces from the old system were starting to appear on the MVR's public platforms wearing the obligatory red berets – often to mask their own past and their opportunistic intentions.

What Chávez offered was a promise of an authentic democracy – not the sham democracy of alternating parties of which Washington was so enamoured, but a rejection of neo-liberalism, an egalitarian redistribution of Venezuela's oil wealth, a recognition of the rights of women and of minority indigenous and Afro-Venezuelan communities, and a military that served the people.

Chávez won 56.2 per cent of the popular vote, a stunning victory by any standards. The barrios exploded, using up the rockets they would normally keep for the New Year's celebration. Roland Denis, wandering the city, saw 'the people enormously happy, dancing and drinking … Caracas looked beautiful, full of lights, car horns and music. I had never seen it so happy.'

Chávez was officially sworn in in February 1999. The chief justice administered the swearing in and a cavernous Rafael Caldera, his face oozing disapproval, handed over the presidential sash. Chávez's two-hour acceptance speech was unlike any previous ones. From the microphone he announced:'I swear before my people upon this moribund constitution that I will drive forward the necessary democratic transformations so that the new republic will have a Magna Carta befitting these new times.'

True to his word, his first act, that same month, was to organise a referendum on whether to elect a Constituent Assembly to draft a new constitution. In April 88 per cent of the electorate supported the proposal and in July 91 per cent voted for the 131 delegates: 119 of them were Chavistas, including Chávez's wife, his brother, and five of his ministers. The Assembly met and produced at extraordinary speed a draft new constitution to be voted on in a referendum on 15 December.

As people queued to cast their votes in Caracas and the neighbouring state of Vargas, the rain that had fallen for nearly three weeks intensified. The Avila mountain that overlooks the city was covered with a thick mist. On the night of the 15/16 December the mountain began to move and a torrent of mud rocks washed down over the port of La Guaira and the state of Vargas, engulfing everything its path – fragile shanties and middle-class housing alike. Those who died in the disaster were never finally counted, but 100,000 is the figure usually cited.

The damage amounted to 2,500 million Bolívars. There was a terrible irony in it, in that Bolívar had faced a massive earthquake in 1812, just after a victory. And like Bolívar, Chávez had also been challenged by a leader of the church, suggesting that this was the vengeance of God or Nature. Bolívar had replied, 'then we will fight Nature too'. Chávez's more melancholy response was to remind the Archbishop of Caracas, Ignacio Velasco, that, 'Nature sometimes reminds us that we do not have absolute power'.

Chávez's reaction to the tragedy did him great credit; he personally organised the response, constantly moving from community to community and visibly getting very little sleep. And he immediately implemented his Plan Bolívar 2000, mobilising the army to respond to the disaster; the plan envisaged a more clearly social role for the military and this was its first expression.

The new Constitution was passed with a majority of 71 per cent, and the new National Assembly which replaced the bicameral legislature that preceded it, in imitation of the US Congress and Senate. The new Constitution held to its undertaking to guarantee rights across the board, to investigate and transform the notorious corrupt Venezuelan legal system, to provide checks and balances to control public officials, including the provision that allowed for a referendum to recall them at the mid-way point of their tenure. It also changed the name of the country, to the Bolivarian Republic, which predictably enough enraged the right wing. And it also provided for the possibility of a two-term presidency (each lasting six years). An early resolution to the Assembly calling for a reform of the corrupt Venezuelan Labour Congress (CTV), however, was vetoed by the Assembly's first president, Luis Miquilena. As Chávez reminds us, 'Until 1996 we had chosen not to participate in the elections. Really, we were calling for abstention as the tactical element in a strategy to force a constitutional assembly, which was always our plan.'[2]

In fact, that is not the whole picture. The members of MBR-200 had only been won to the plan to stand in elections with great difficulty and after Chávez had threatened to resign if his view was not given the organisation's backing. The decision to stand was driven by his alliance with elements of the old order, albeit radical ones, like the Medina wing of Causa R (including Alí Rodríguez Araque, Aristóbulo Istúriz and others) and the MAS (from which his economic adviser Jorge Giordani came), but without the group's historic leaders Teodoro Petkoff and Domingo Alberto Rangel. It was certainly the wily Luis Miquilena who had the greatest sway over him; he had been instrumental in winning Chávez to an electoral strategy. Miquilena was an old communist and a political operator of considerable skill, having survived within the *puntofijista* system since its inception.

The tensions within the MVR, the Movement of the Fifth Republic that was the political expression of the electoral alliance, were not resolved by the election victory, however; it remained a tactical alliance uniting radically disparate views of what the Bolivarian

proceso – not a revolution, but a revolutionary process through time
– could mean.

Chávez in the World

In a speech in May 1999 Chávez movingly set out the reasons for the
sense of urgency that had moved him into the electoral arena.

> … Today this society is falling apart; there's a small part of it
> enjoying opulence, a middle class that can't hold it together and a
> major part of the society that is marginal and marginalised living
> in appalling poverty, without work, and in chaos. The society has
> been falling to pieces, deteriorating. And the same is happening
> in politics, in ethics, and in social relations … The political
> system has collapsed, the powers of the State have disintegrated
> … And it's the same in the economy, because there has been an
> implacable, relentless process of degeneration over four decades
> which, thank God, are now coming to an end and we are starting
> again … Either we integrate and unite in one world or we will
> be overwhelmed by that evil globalization, that globalization that
> imposes itself on others, that dominates and controls, that wants a
> unipolar world. No the world cannot be unipolar or even bipolar,
> it must be multipolar.[3]

Integration would be a permanent theme of Chávez's Bolivarian
discourse – and not only Latin American integration, Bolívar's
pan-American vision. In his first year in office, Chávez spent over
50 days travelling the world in the elderly Boeing 737 which would
finally collapse a year and a half later. He met with Bill Clinton in the
US, visited the Yankee Stadium and pitched the opening ball at Shea
Stadium. He knelt before the Pope in the Vatican. Towards the end
of his first year he travelled to Asia with 100 compatriots, meeting
Chinese president Jiang Zemin and jogging along the Chinese Wall.
These visits were partly diplomatic, a way of putting Venezuela
(and Chávez) on the map and taking the first steps in the creation
of a multipolar world. There were also more practical purposes
behind his travelling – the revival of OPEC (the organisation of

oil-producing countries founded in 1961 by an earlier Venezuelan oil minister, Juan Pablo Pérez Alfonso), which had not met since the 1970s, and the rebuilding of the organisation that could win equity in the international oil trade. And in the longer view, and albeit it was not yet articulated as such, Chávez was setting out to demonstrate an alternative internationalism, a coalition of national states resisting the invasions of the global market, or at the very least defining their relationship with the global system. That was probably his original contribution to Bolívar's concept of integration.

The conservative opposition denounced his relentless travelling as grandstanding, as a sign of overweening ambition. And indeed in his first three years in power, Chávez spent 170 days outside Venezuela, visiting 71 countries.[4] Besides the more practical motives for his journeying, he also made an impact in other ways. He was a curious mixture of respect for ritual, particularly the religious and the military, and an almost childish delight in breaking protocol. His karate stance with Putin, his flirtation with Rosario Green, the Mexican foreign minister, his embrace of the Japanese emperor, all contributed to an image of endearing naivete. In Venezuela his challenges to the formalities of international diplomacy went down well. But they also added to an enigma that he may have created deliberately. Was he a serious international leader, or a self-deluding populist? Or was he consciously appealing to the movements arising across the world in the wake of the Seattle demonstrations against the WTO late in 1999. The demonstrations coincided with his China visit – though he will have found no sympathy for them among the Chinese rulers. His emphasis on democracy, and his suspicion of party politics, however, certainly resonated with the new anti-capitalist mood.

The immediate priority, however, was to redress the negative impact of the preceding years of neo-liberal austerity. Although Jorge Giordani's longer-term economic plan involved developing Venezuela's agricultural and industrial sectors to undermine its dependency on oil, in the immediate action Chávez had undertaken to set in motion social welfare programmes to improve the health and education systems immediately, and to address some urgent problems of infrastructure. His Plan Bolívar gave the army the task of developing the projects, building roads and schools and so on. It was a sensible way to use military labour constructively and a visible and palpable demonstration of the new role the military could play in a progressive society. The immediate investment was $113 million, but this was clearly a fraction of what would be required to restore the living standards so brutally undermined in the previous decade. The key to realising the Bolivarian welfare promise was, of course, oil.

When Chávez came to power the price of oil was at rock bottom – at $8.43 a barrel. This was a direct consequence of the way in which the oil corporation, Pdvsa, had been run in the past, and particularly since the 'internationalisation' process implemented in 1983. Essentially, 'the goal of shifting profits abroad was the real motive for internationalisation'.[5] It transferred its profits towards its US operation, Citgo, and to the other companies with whom it had 'operating agreements'. For 18 years after internationalisation, Pdvsa's foreign affiliates paid not a single cent into the Venezuelan exchequer. In his campaigning Chávez had frequently declared that Pdvsa would have to be brought under control, that the royalties paid should be far higher than they were, and that this essential resource should be run by the state for the national good. For the United States, to whom Venezuela supplied some 15 per cent of its oil needs, this sounded ominous. And it was clearly the case that Chávez's whole economic policy and his promise to reverse the neo-liberal strategy and increase social spending was predicated on increasing oil revenues, and keeping them within the country. Nonetheless he went to great lengths to reassure Washington that he would continue to supply the US and welcome foreign capital; to make the point he even rang the bell at the New York Stock Exchange on his US trip. Clinton and Bush, unsurprisingly, insisted that oil prices were too high (at $8 a barrel!), but for Chávez it was an immediate priority to raise them, to finance his ambitious social programmes.

By the late 1990s, however, and faced with Chávez's threat to its continuing independence from the state, Pdvsa began to act in a more overtly political role. Its methods and practices were ideological expressions of neo-liberalism, since economic impulses control political behaviour in the global market. It was not just that they acted like any other multinational company; they saw their role as working to impose the invisible hand of the market in every area.

Luis Giusti, Pdvsa's president, was unapologetic about his presidential ambitions – and there was a logic in it, given the determination of the right wing to continue the austerity policies imposed by the IMF and to complete the process of privatisation.

Although Chávez welcomed foreign private investment, and undertook to pay the foreign debt (after initially threatening to refuse), it was a reflection of the urgency of Venezuela's need for capital. The core of any future plan must address the price of oil, and this had to be done through OPEC. In fact, however, its ability to control oil prices and production levels among its members had been weakened, not least by Pdvsa's open refusal to adhere to quotas, arguing instead to increase production. According to Bernard Mommer, Pdvsa was largely responsible for bringing OPEC to the verge of collapse before Chávez's timely intervention. His voice and representative in OPEC was Alí Rodríguez Araque. He had been a guerrilla commander and a member of Causa R, before joining the PPT and the Chávez government. Rodríguez Araque had been Causa R's oil expert, and from 1999 onwards he would play a key role in oil policy, as well as many other areas of Chávez's economic and social policies.

The two men were a dramatic contrast. The flamboyant Chávez made his public impact on the world very quickly and very successfully. Rodríguez Araque, for all his radical past, was a quiet and serious man, his words always measured and careful. He was, and is, as still and thoughtful as Chávez was dynamic and spontaneous. The combination proved very successful. The two men began to restore quotas in order to stabilise, and ultimately increase, oil prices. In September 2000 they hosted a summit meeting of OPEC heads of state in Caracas, and oil prices moved beyond $20. At the same time, Rodríguez Araque reimposed the requirement that oil companies pay royalties, calculated on the basis of volume and price only, for both oil and gas. This countermanded the fact that Pdvsa had previously introduced which included the provision that no company could be required to pay double taxes. Pdvsa for its part invested a large proportion of its own profits abroad, and operating expenses were deducted from what it paid at home. In fact in the previous 20 years its contribution to the Venezuelan exchequer had declined from

71 per cent of its earnings to 24 per cent. To all intents and purposes Pdvsa had acted throughout the decade as an autonomous entity, a state within a state. If it was to be the engine of economic and social change that Chávez hoped it would become, therefore, that situation could not persist. And the confrontation that that implied would come soon enough.

Ambiguities

Hugo Chávez had won the presidency as the candidate of the Movement of the Fifth Republic (MVR). But this fifth republic contained different and contradictory currents, whose internal tensions would soon emerge. At this stage, Chávez was representing radicals, revolutionaries, as well as established left organisations whose expectations were, in many cases, ambiguous. This, after all, was a revolution which promised to pay the foreign debt and which had the support of the country's leading media baron, Cisneros, and the leading newspaper, *El Nacional*. Washington seemed to be holding its fire at first, especially when Chávez guaranteed the continuing supply of Venezuelan oil to the US,[6] while the US ambassador in Caracas had urged the State Department to pay less attention to what Chávez said and more to his actions. On the other hand, the Church, the employers' organisation Fedecámaras and the Pdvsa management quickly 'stepped into the vacuum created by the loss of credibility of the two parties that had governed Venezuela for 40 years'.[7]

The conflicts soon emerged around the Constituent Assembly and the proposals on Pdvsa, for the legalisation of abortion, for changes to the social security system and other controversial issues. Chávez urged moderation on his delegates, withdrawing the abortion proposal, for example, in deference to the Catholic Church. The chair of the Assembly was Luis Miquilena, the consummate pragmatist whose domination of the complexities of machine politics had clearly impressed Chávez. Within the MVR the emerging rivalries focused on the excessive power wielded by Miquilena. The announcement of the candidacy of Arias Cárdenas, with whom Chávez had often disagreed and who had been a member of Causa R, for the 2000 presidential election exposed another, and important, division.

Arias Cárdenas had long been critical of Chávez's ambitions, and as governor of the oil-rich state of Zulia he had real influence. In a well-publicised incident, Arias presented Chávez with a chicken as an allusion to his alleged cowardice in the 4 February coup. His other key ally in the founding of the MBR, and indeed from the very earliest conspiratorial meetings, Jesús Urdaneta, also fell out with him very badly in 2000. Urdaneta was appointed by Chávez to head Disip, the state security agency. When it was accused of shooting looters during the Vargas disasters, he was forced to resign.

Urdaneta bitterly complained that he was being forced out by Chávez's allies, and that the attack on him was a cover for corruption within the administration of the disaster funds. A third original member of the MBR, Yael Acosta Chirinos, joined his two comrades at a press conference on the eighth anniversary of their coup (in February 2000), to denounce Chávez's excessive dependence on Miquilena and veteran journalist (and erstwhile presidential candidate) José Vicente Rangel, alleging corruption and cynical opportunism against both. The three shared the view, expressed in the angry exchanges at the 1997 MBR congress, that the military should have a leading role in the political process. Indeed the right wing had been extremely critical of the clauses in the new constitution that accorded greater autonomy to the military and of the large number of military officers in Chávez's first Cabinet. As the editor of NACLA warned in advance of the 2000 elections, 'Internal democracy and ideological clarity are two imperatives that Chávez and his MVR can no longer ignore'. It was a well-timed warning, but it was not addressed at the time and remained a problem throughout the Chávez decade.

There was a profound contradiction at work here, which was not widely discussed. At every step, change came as a result of Chávez's direct personal intervention, and of his own individual decisions. 'I made the announcement (of the dissolution of the MVR) as a result of a reflection process that did not involve consulting with or debate within the party. I remember when I made the announcement I got a standing ovation ... The main point in my talk was about the need to regenerate the movement of the masses.'[8]

Having created a political instrument that did not have that ability, Chávez was placing himself above and outside it in order to mobilise support for his initiatives. In the name of the mass movement he was at this stage reinforcing the centrality of his own role in the process. It may be argued that in the absence of an organised Bolivarian *movement* it was his historic responsibility to assume a role of leadership in this way. But the impact on the organs of mass struggle which had existed and developed in the previous few years and which had identified with Chávez was to increasingly narrow their scope for initiatives and independent action. And there was always an alternative that he could have opted for – to build those organisations in the hope that they would become the political leadership of tomorrow.

The first year of his administration showed Chávez in several different lights. The different aspects of his personality would continue to confuse and divide commentators on both sides of the widening political divide. It was clear that he had changed and would continue to change. Yet his tremendous impact both on Venezuela and on Latin America had to do with the combination of his personality and his circumstances – and so too did the contradictions that caused so much comment. Chávez had defined himself by his distance from all prior political definitions – that was his strength. That he did *not* belong to any recognisable political tradition nor represent directly any collective interests in his own society. In a sense that was his attraction on the global stage as well. The playful antics that disoriented the monarchs and leaders he encountered, especially in his first year and a half of office, were partly the signs of a playful character who was fond of jokes and stories, like most *llaneros*. But it was also an affirmation and a reminder that he was different, and that precisely was his appeal. His consummate skill as a communicator emerged in the course of the campaign and afterwards in a way that had not been obvious before then. It certainly won him the election, and he sought consciously to build on it in his first year of office. He established a newspaper, *El correo del presidente*, started a radio programme and launched his first attempt at a regular television slot (*De frente con el presidente*), all in 1999. None was a success, but they were a precedent for what would later become a permanent feature of Venezuelan political life, the open-ended Sunday morning programme, *Aló Presidente*.

The right wing condemned his media activities as populism. But the communications industry was dominated by powerful conservative forces who very quickly turned vehemently against Chávez, attacking his policies and constantly and systematically undermining him because of his social and ethnic background. But for his core base of supporters, it was an attack on them and only served to reinforce their backing for *el comandante*. In 2000, Chávez continued his restless journeyings, but he was also preparing a series of new laws under the 'Ley Habilitante' which gave him authority to push through laws from the presidential office.[9] That the MVR did not have a two-thirds majority in the new National Assembly made that necessary. But it also served to feed the rising anger of the right against what they saw as an authoritarian direction given legitimacy by the right to presidential re-election for two terms (now increased from five to six years each under the new Constitution). It was Chávez's assessment that it would be the minimum required to carry through the changes he envisaged to complete what he called *el proceso*. The old order, however, still had powerful bulwarks in the state, the judiciary, the army and the church, as well as the media; although the new constitution strengthened the presidential prerogative even more, it did not – despite relentless conservative affirmations to the contrary – permit Chávez to challenge or reorganise the state machine itself. He could have done so, of course, but Chávez was and remained firmly committed to the democratic system as amended.

It was hard to deny, even recognising the degree of hostile propaganda that was now pouring from the media at home and abroad, that Chávez was very publicly enjoying the trappings of power. After the collapse of his old presidential aircraft, much was made of his £65 million purchase of the French Airbus; in fact it was a relatively modest purchase. But there were signs of a certain weakness. He began to wear expensive designer suits and elegant watches. In itself this may have meant little, except that Chávez was reputed to have no interest in material things. (The same could not be said of his family.) Until the very moment of his election he had lived extremely modestly, often in other people's houses; he ate where he could and preferred the traditional food of ordinary Venezuelans – *arepas*, beans, fried banana and, above all, coffee. He now also began to wear a uniform (as President he was also Commander in Chief) and on one occasion at least, on the anniversary of Pérez Jiménez's overthrow, a full-dress white uniform complete with medals. Yet Chávez had resigned from the army after the February coup. It was a sign of his enduring loyalty to the military, as well as a certain enjoyment of some of the rituals of government.

Yet in a speech in April 1999 he had said:

> Without an awakened people, in full consciousness and in action, no revolution is possible. There are no Messiahs, no 'caudillos' who can lead a revolutionary process. The people are the sine qua non of any revolutionary process.

> If we fail the people, if we do not help it to organise itself, if the people do not find their own historical consciousness, then we are lost, then we will be like Sisyphus, cursed to push a rock to the top of a mountain but then, as he neared the top, the rock began to roll back and he was condemned to begin again .. .and so on, for years and years ... .[10]

The emphasis on the central role (*protagonismo*) of the mass movement was a constant theme of Chávez's speeches in those early years, together with the repeated warning that this was a process over time. His eloquence and his ability to speak directly, even from a television screen, were evidenced when *Aló Presidente* began broadcasting in May 1999. For many observers, the programme was slightly absurd – Chávez was not avuncular like Franklin Roosevelt in his fireside chats; it was rumbustious, sometimes long-winded and chaotic in its improvisation. From an early stage Chávez would have his ministers sit in the front row of whatever location had been chosen for that week; their apprehensive faces were testimony to Chávez's habit of announcing new policies, without warning, and then addressing the relevant minister with questions and instructions.

As criticisms of the MVR and its functioning increased, and evidence began to accumulate of the corruption of Miquilena and José Vicente Rangel, and as the inevitable sycophants began to gather around an ingenuous Chávez, the president finally acknowledged the problem, and revived the near defunct MBR. Some of those who had enjoyed the fruits of power began to withdraw their support, prime among them Miquilena, who ostentatiously distanced himself from Chávez before eventually resigning in early 2002, still declaring, unconvincingly, his continuing support for Chávez.

There was no doubt that Chávez's proposals were radical and that they enjoyed the enthusiastic support of the millions of Venezuelans who had elected him to his first six-year presidency. At the same time, within the MVR and the Polo Patriótico, the fragile unity was breaking down to reveal the conflicts beneath the surface. Alfredo Peña, elected first on the list to the Constituent Assembly and to the National Assembly thereafter, complained of the slow pace of privatisation. Miquilena was distancing himself from Chávez in the face of his shift to the left, as he saw it. The MVR, then, could not be the political instrument to drive forward these new policies, especially since it functioned largely as a bureaucratic layer with no activist base. Faced with this, Chávez moved away from his old allies and took an individual decision to dissolve the MVR and replace it, possibly with a reconstituted MBR.

Chávez now went to the country for the second presidential election of his career, in May 2000, under the terms of the new Constitution. In the event, and despite the bitter hostility of the media and the persistent rumours of corruption – which has a particularly powerful resonance in Venezuela after 40 years of puntofijismo – Chávez emerged with an increased majority. He won 60 per cent of the vote. The irony was that while he laid enormous emphasis on participatory democracy and the rights and demands of the people, the Chavista regime was by no means unfriendly to capital – domestic or foreign. The *Financial Times* had commended his management of the economy through its first 100 days and while he denounced neo-liberalism in general, he amended that to hostility to *savage* neo-liberalism after a visit to the Vatican. Furthermore, the 1999 Constitution explicitly protected private property. This tension runs throughout the Constitution, and throughout the Bolivarian process. The gestures in the direction of a popular democracy, the affirmation of collective rather than individual rights, are revolutionary promises. The creation of a welfare state of some kind, based on the appropriation and distribution of oil revenues – the idea of 'sowing the seeds of oil' (*sembrar el petróleo*) first voiced by the conservative historian Arturo Uslar Pietri – would represent a massive improvement in the lives of the majority of Venezuelans. But it was not a socialist revolution, the redistribution of the wealth and power of the capitalist class among the society as a whole. And the increasing centralisation of power in the President was also in conflict with the promise of a participatory democracy in which the people are the governors of their own lives through the democratic organs that grow up in the course of social struggle.

The confusion, and the difficulty of characterising Hugo Chávez and his project is that he managed to stand astride both elements, for some considerable time at least. For many of his colleagues and allies in the MVR, their vision was of a reconstituted and relegitimated state rebuilt out of the ruins of the old. The 'Ley Habilitante' or Enabling Law allowed Chávez to push through the next phase of his project in mid-2001. It often seemed that the proposals coming from the presidential palace were improvised, and tested in practice. In 1999 a network of popular education groups had formed an Education Constituent Assembly to develop a proposal for a new education system that would reflect the values of Chavismo. When the new education law, drafted by the revolutionary and ex-guerrilla Carlos Lanz, was published it drove the middle classes wild. With encouragement from the mass media they were mobilised on to the streets, denouncing the proposal as Cuban-influenced, communist and a blueprint for indoctrination. Hundreds of thousands took to the streets in protest and in defence of private education – the first major mobilisation of the right. Chávez was scathing in his responses. It was an example of the rhetoric outstripping action that would often repeat itself. Eventually the law was withdrawn, though not the commitment to improving public education. But the central pieces of legislation concerned the oil industry, and the media. Marcano and Tyszka argue[11] that Chávez's obsession with the media and particularly television was an indication that he was the first Venezuelan president to have been a child of the TV age. That is certainly true, but it is also true that in the 'guided democracy' that

Venezuela had been for so long, political propaganda substituted for genuine political debate, and patronage for the democratic allocation of public power. That was the method into which Venezuelans had been educated and against which Chávez set out to communicate his contrary project for mass participation and involvement. Chávez had seen how he had been treated by the mass media previously, and especially during the election campaign, and he resolved to challenge, and at times to provoke them.

The other law, establishing direct state control over Pdvsa, was the kernel of his economic and social policy. He and Rodríguez Araque had succeeded in re-energizing OPEC, re-establishing quotas, and raising the market price. The gathering of OPEC in 2000 had been both a political and an economic triumph. But the other element of Bolivarian oil policy was to redistribute these increased oil revenues across society. First, however, Pdvsa had to be taken back into state control and its existing executives removed. The new plan could hardly be administered by the same team, under Luis Giusti, that had effectively privatised the corporation in 1995 and signed operating agreements with foreign multinationals that allowed them to pay virtually nothing to the Venezuelan government (on the grounds that they already paid tax in their home countries). Furthermore in the increasingly conflictive atmosphere of 2001, Pdvsa was playing a direct political role together with the employers' organisation Fedecámaras, the Church, and the powerful capitalist groups like Cisneros, the Capriles and the Zuloagas. Chávez's response was to launch the Bolivarian Circles, grassroots organs of around twelve people who would monitor the political environment locally and mobilise support for him.

On 10 December 2001, the Venezuelan Congress of Labour (CTV), led by the notoriously corrupt Carlos Ortega, called a national strike, ostensibly around a 40 per cent wage demand. It had the immediate backing of the employers' organisation and the Pdvsa directors. In reality it was a reaction to the proposed changes to Pdvsa, under the Enabling Law, and a clear shot across Chávez's bows. Its longer term purpose was his removal. It would become clear later that it was in some sense a rehearsal. And since the workers who withdrew their labour that day were paid by their employers, it was clear that this was a lockout, a bosses strike to test the water. The CTV, after all, was a key instrument of the *puntofijista* state, and as corrupt as its other institutions. The lockout failed, despite the support of a number of capitalist enterprises and the backing of the media, for whom it was part of a pattern of slow Cubanisation. The first Cuban medical personnel had recently arrived and the newly formed Bolivarian Circles were modelled, it was asserted, on the Cuban Committees for the Defence of the Revolution.

It cannot have been unconnected that Chávez had reacted to 9/11 by expressing sympathy for the victims but then famously, in his *Aló Presidente* programme, showing photographs of wounded Afghan children and warning Bush that 'you cannot fight terrorism with terrorism'. Colin Powell responded by publicly criticising Chávez's visits to Gaddafi and Saddam Hussein, to which Chávez testily responded by asking what gave the US the right to tell him what to do. And departing US ambassador Hrinak used his farewell speech to criticise Chávez for his excessive closeness to the Colombian Farc. 'I hoped to see a true revolution in Venezuela', he said. 'Real changes, a more efficient public administration, less corruption, more economic development, more opportunities for the people. I have seen none of that.'[12] It must be one of the very rare occasions on which a US ambassador has lamented the absence of revolution – though his masters had made their own contribution to preventing it, and had now declared openly their hostility to the Bolivarian process.

In January 2002, Luis Miquilena finally made public his break with Chávez. It was only one of a number of splits that had riven the the electoral alliance, the Polo Patriótico, as it divided over attitudes to Chávez. They cited his militarism, his excessive centralisation of power on the one hand, and his moves to the left and his closeness to Cuba on the other. The alliance was breaking down, as Chávez raised the tone of his challenge to the right-wing opposition. His TV broadcasts were lengthening; the 100th *Aló Presidente*, in March, established a record, at seven hours and 35 minutes. Then in early April he pulled out a whistle, shouted 'Offside' and announced the dismissal of a long list of Pdvsa executives.

The Revolution is Televised

2002 was a year of confrontation. The opposition demonstrations began to increase in frequency and intensity from 23 January onwards. On 4 February, 600,000 marched through Caracas to commemorate the 1992 coup. A week later, Guaicaipuro Lameda, the military man appointed by Chávez 18 months earlier to the presidency of Pdvsa, was sacked; although Lameda had been a member of the MBR, he was now clearly allied to the so-called 'meritocracy', as the management of Pdvsa were known. Chávez's replacement nominees entered a battleground. The existing management prevaricated while it drew up a plan to resist the government's attempts to carry through their removal. Its proposals included organising street demonstrations, sabotaging production and using the media to discredit Chávez. By late March, the plan began to be implemented. The first step was the shut down of the massive El Palito refinery on 4 April, with the collusion of the CTV leadership. By the 6th, the CIA was reporting that a group of dissident military officers was conspiring with others to bring about the overthrow of Chávez. The first step would be to provoke confrontations and violence in the streets.[13] The CTV called another national strike for 9 April, two days after Chávez had blown his famous whistle. On that day, while the right wing claimed a full walkout, the reality was that about 30 per cent of workers had stopped work. Chávez in a day long *cadena* – a national government broadcast that all channels were obliged to show – compared the strategies adopted by the right to the two bosses strikes that preceded the overthrow of Salvador Allende in Chile on 11 September 1973.[14]

The comparison with Chile is a valid one. There the government of Popular Unity under Allende was elected in late 1970 with a programme of social reforms and a peaceful transition to socialism. The response of the Chilean bourgeosie was to mobilise its economic power, and its influence among the military, as well as the shock troops of the Fatherland and Freedom organisation whose base lay among small businessmen like the lorry owner-drivers. Its principal weapon was the creation of shortages of goods to destabilise Allende's regime, and then to launch national strikes that divided the working-class movement. All this, which the right-wing opposition in Chile described as a 'soft coup', was designed to create insecurity and instability, weakening the state before the final stage, the direct military assault on Allende in the presidential palace. These were clearly the two phases envisaged by the anti-Chávez movement – first the instability and the economic assault, then the military intervention to 'restore order'. On the tenth Ortega of the Trade Union Congress (CTV) and the dull head of the employers organisation Fedecámaras, Pedro Carmona, jointly announced an indefinite strike – a rare example of management and workers agreeing to jointly support a reactionary proposal.

A right-wing protest march was then called for 10 a.m. on the morning of the 11th to march from the offices of Pdvsa in the east of the city to the CTV offices near what was then the Hilton Hotel at Bellas Artes in the city centre. The leaders of the protest were not in fact marching – they were gathered for a working breakfast in the Hilton. From there the message went out to march on to Miraflores, the presidential palace down the long Avenida Mexico, for which permission had already been refused. In fact foreign correspondents had been informed the day before that this would happen. It was a provocation which could only lead to violence. Chavistas were marching down the two avenues parallel to the route of the opposition march, then turning on to the Avenida Baralt to march towards the presidential palace. The avenue passes under a bridge, but as the Chavista march moved towards it, shots rang out. Several people were killed and others climbed the stair to reach the refuge of the bridge. From the opposite direction but at some distance, the opposition march was also approaching. The Metropolitan Police, under the orders of opposition supporters Peña (governor of greater Caracas) and López (mayor of the conservative district of Chacao), were sent to Baralt Avenue with explicit orders to fire on demonstrators who, it was said, were firing at the opposition. The explanation sent around the world that afternoon was that Chávez supporters had fired on the opposition, and severely doctored newsreels reinforced that impression. As we now know, the shots were fired by snipers on the roof of the Eden Hotel, beside the bridge, and the man photographed firing his pistol from the bridge was a government supporter firing back at them.[15]

The result was a massacre, but the opposition was well prepared and their strategy was ready for implementation. The denunciation of the events at Puente Llaguno, which then became the reason to remove Chávez from power, cannot have been known at 1.15 when General Ramírez Pérez recorded his televised message reporting that six people had been killed. The march did not reach that point until 3.10. Nevertheless the strategy agreed over lunch by Ortega, Lameda (the recently fired head of Pdvsa), Pedro Carmona of Fedecámaras and Cisneros[16] the powerful head of television company Venevisión, was already under way.

Chávez himself was in Miraflores, broadcasting to the country on state television. The private television channels split their screen to show the Puente Llaguno shootings beside pictures of the presidential broadcast. Significantly Chávez appears in military uniform – and we now know that he had already set in motion his Plan Avila, an emergency plan to mobilise the armed forces to maintain public order. But by then the dissident right-wing officers had redirected traffic from the nearby motorway to the main garrison, Fuerte Tiuna, to prevent troops from getting out – and the mayor of Chacao, Leopoldo López, was taking keys from drivers on the motorway to further paralyse the city. Inside Fuerte Tiuna, Chávez's most reliable ally, General García Carneiro, was detained by brother officers. By 9.30 all lines of communication from the presidential palace had been severed. Chávez gathered his closest collaborators around him and asked for their view of the situation. His vice-president, José Vicente Rangel, was adamant that they had to resist. Others recommended negotiation. Just after midnight, Fidel Castro called Chávez. His advice was clear – don't let yourself be destroyed. Don't resign, and seek honourable terms of surrender. By dawn, Chávez had accepted the situation and agreed to negotiate, fearful perhaps of the bloodshed that might result if he did not. The task now was to inform the people, agree to leave the country, and guarantee the safety of those he left behind.

It may have been the early hours of the morning when Chávez made his decision, but Venezuela was not sleeping. The happy accident of the presence in Caracas of a film crew from RTE (Ireland) has left us with an extraordinary and unique record of what happened in the palace of Miraflores when Chávez was detained and taken to Fuerte Tiuna.[17] A crowd gathers inside the palace with champagne in hand to celebrate the fall of Chávez. The head of Fedecámaras, the employers' organisation, Pedro Carmona, hardly a charismatic figure, now modestly allows himself to be nominated as the new president – and removes from his pocket an orange presidential sash he just happened to be carrying. The atmosphere in the palace is hysterical, as the Irish film documentary shows to brilliant effect. The demon has gone and the removal of all Chávez's officials is announced to those present, who include many high ranking military officers and the Cardinal. The Bolivarian Constitution will immediately be suspended. The next morning television newsreaders will read out lists of names of leading Chávez supporters who are to be arrested or killed. The police and security forces, however, had already moved into action and a number of people were already dead, 30 of them executed by the state security police, Disip. In the middle-class suburb of Altamira, the Cuban embassy is under siege; the crowd, led by the future right-wing presidential candidate Henrique Capriles, cuts off the electricity and water supplies to the embassy and smashes up cars in the street belonging to embassy employees. Leading members of the Chávez regime are detained by crowds in the street, and beaten. Carmona's announcement from Miraflores of the suspension of all rights and the appointment of a new army high command does not go down well, however, even among his own allies. General Vazquez Velazco, for example, has been a leading conspirator – yet he is passed over. And officers loyal to Chávez are actively exploiting the discontent among the armed forces. In Caracas García Carneiro returns to Fuerte Tiuna; in Maracay, General Baduel's Parachute regiment is holding firm.

Chávez meanwhile was still being held in Fuerte Tiuna, but he was given no information about what was planned for him until he was told that he was to be moved. Chávez was clearly afraid; convinced that he was about to be killed, he prayed as the plane he boarded flew the 40 minutes to Turiamo naval base. From there he was taken to the island naval base at La Orchila; his assumption was that he would then be flown out of the country. Among the soldiers there was obvious sympathy for Chávez, though the structure of command did not allow that sympathy to find active expression – except that is for one young guard who agreed to smuggle out a note. It said, simply, 'Turiamo, April 13th 2.45 p.m. To the Venezuelan people. I have not resigned'.

The resignation issue was critical. From the moment he arrived at Fuerte Tiuna, Chávez was under pressure to sign a pre-prepared resignation letter. He refused. He was leaving, he said, but he had not and would not resign – and therefore what had occurred on the previous day was not a change of government but an illegitimate military coup. The note reached General Baduel and Chávez's wife, Marisabel, who had gone to Barquisimeto with her children, broadcast the news through Cuban television – it was then retransmitted by CNN.

The balance of forces was changing dramatically as these things were happening. And it was not as a result of negotiations or secret messages. The Irish documentary on the coup shows how the situation was being transformed.

The camera pans from the smiling, self-congratulating leaders of the coup, toasting one another in champagne, to the windows of Miraflores looking out on to the Avenida Urdaneta beyond. The palace is surrounded as the barrios flood down from the hills. 'El pueblo', the people, are besieging the palace demanding the return of Chávez. Their red baseball caps and t-shirts, their dark skins and their raised voices, announce who they are. Their slogans and shouts articulate their demands. The same thing is happening elsewhere. In Maracay, the parachute regiment's base is surrounded by Chavistas supporting Baduel.

The frozen smiles of Carmona and his friends are eloquent. They had assumed that only two actors were occupying the historical stage – Hugo Chávez, and themselves. Now a third protagonist had entered the scenario and changed the script. Outside Miraflores were gathered the social movements and organisations that had supported Chávez and carried him to the presidency, the 'pueblo soberano' – a sovereign people exercising its power directly and imposing, by its very presence, a new and different political logic – the power of the people.

Events moved swiftly thereafter. On the morning of the 13th the US and Spanish ambassadors met with Carmona – Bush and Aznar, the Spanish Prime Minister had already issued a joint declaration supporting the coup. At midday Baduel called a press conference in Maracay. An hour later Miraflores was retaken and at Fuerte Tiuna a meeting of officers agreed to restore the Constitution. Carmona sought refuge in Fuerte Tiuna before eventually fleeing to Colombia. He was known from then on as Pedro the Brief – for obvious reasons. By now, one million people have gathered at Miraflores. At 7 p.m., Diosdado Cabello, vice president, arrived to assume formal control of government. At 2 a.m. the helicopters arrived at La Orchila that would return Chávez to his post. On his arrival at Miraflores, he spoke to a delirious waiting crowd from the balcony of the presidential palace.

Figure 5.1 Chávez addresses the crowd from the balcony at Miraflores, the presidential palace (© Luis Noguera)

His speech was measured and conciliatory. 'There will be no reprisals here, no persecution, no abuses of power, no offences against freedom of expression or thought, or human rights in general....now it has been shown that this people's consciousness of its own strength has awoken and it has become an actor on the historical stage forging its own path... '

His final call was for unity, naming each sector of society in turn and calling on each to work for a united Bolivarian Venezuela.

It was a modest but brilliant speech, in which Chávez promised to rethink things and to learn the lessons of these 48 hours.

The majority of analysts of these events see the loyal officers and soldiers as the key to the coup's failure. These same commentators see the crowds in the street as mere interested spectators not, as Chávez put it, as the subjects of their own history. Yet embedded in Chávez's Bolivarian discourse was the concept of a new democracy, participatory and collective; that was always one of the currents at the heart of the Bolivarian idea. To see the soldiers as the key actors is to sustain an explanation that sees the leaders as the subjects of history. Yet during these extraordinary 48 hours it was the mass movement that acted without hesitation, and defeated the coup, and the leaders who followed. Chávez's speech from the balcony seemed to recognise that, and it would inform the next, radical phase of the Bolivarian revolution.

What happened in those two days in April was that the course of events came to be determined by new forces, whose entry on to the stage of history changed the balance of power in Venezuela. The masses who filled the streets were not merely spectators, they were actors. The old ruling class could not conceive of the people of Venezuela as anything other than clients, pawns moved from above, makeweights in political processes conducted between politicians claiming to represent them, stage armies moved back and forth at the behest of the powerful. But in April 2002, the powerful were moved *by* them, and their ability to shape events appropriated by the masses gathered outside the presidential palace. And it was not a spontaneous response from millions of individuals, but a collective action mobilised by grassroots organisations. It is in that sense that we can begin to speak here of revolution – the shift of power from one class to another, not instantaneously, of course, but as a process beginning with those events. The concept of *poder popular* became a central theme of political discourse from that point on, though its meaning and forms were yet to be forged.

5

The Bolivarian Revolution Advances

The Bosses Strike

If a revolution is the process of transferring power from one class to another, then those two days in April represented an important new stage in the Bolivarian revolution. In the continuing internal battle between the political currents around Chávez, the attempted coup and its failure had strengthened the participatory current as well as Chávez himself. The creation of the Bolivarian Circles in June 2001 suggested a shift in that direction, though the lack of any clear definition of the political role of the Circles meant that they could be very different things in different places – political units, community education circles, local projects seeking state funding. Many of those who flooded into central Caracas and other cities in the April days will have been mobilised by the Circles in the first six months. According to Guillermo Garcia Ponce, head of the Political Commando of the Revolution, however, there was no plan in place when the April coup took place, despite the intensifying confrontations of the previous months. In fact there was one plan – the Plan Ávila – which Chávez was about to set in motion on the 11th. Significantly, this was a plan for the establishment of military control over the country which flew in the face of the assurances of openness and democratic control from below. Yet despite the increasingly bitter war of words in the early part of 2002, Chávez seemed to hesitate when it came to putting words into action. The Plan would certainly have changed forever the relationship between Chávez and the mass movement.

Politically, Chávez remained committed to constitutional democracy; it was his reference point in every speech and every comment he made on the activities of the opposition. And his appeal from the Miraflores balcony in the early morning of 14 April was to all Venezuelans, for unity and obedience to the constitution. His response to the coup was 'emotional but cautious';[1] he promised to sheathe his sword, suggesting an acknowledgment, implicitly at least, that his own behaviour might have been provocative. He also promised to put away his military uniform. In the days and weeks that followed he was positively conciliatory. Later that year, the Supreme Court, dominated by right wing appointees from the previous era, had adjudged that the military had become involved in the coup because there was a 'vacuum of power' – effectively legitmising the coup. But Chávez refuted their claim, because he had never signed a resignation letter; had he done so, the 'vacuum of power' argument would have given legal cover to those who made the coup. But it was a virtual red light for future military intervention, and the high ranking officers who had been behind the coup largely escaped untouched, though Chávez retired some of the leading figures and promoted in their place others who had been loyal to him.

In the days after the coup Chávez met with a number of people, including Gustavo Cisneros – one of the 'four horsemen of the apocalypse' (as Venezuela's most powerful capitalists were known). Cisneros, as head of Venevisión, had expressed a degree of support for Chávez immediately after his election. That very soon turned into open enmity and active support – or, to be more precise, specifically help in organising – the coup. A witness to the meeting described Cisneros' attitude to Chávez as arrogant and contemptuous, and Chávez's response as apologetic. Cisneros left the meeting unchallenged. He had been present at the Hilton hotel meeting on the 11th, and was in permanent communication with the US government, a task made easy by his membership of the Chase Manhattan Bank's international advisory board and his ownership of the Pepsi-Cola franchise. The US, of course, had rushed to recognise the new regime headed by Carmona. 'After April there was a surprising conservative turn and a conciliatory attitude towards sectors of the oligarchy and the impunity enjoyed by some of those who had made the coup... .'[2]

The fact that most of the military involved escaped punishment, and the continuing hostility (putting it mildly) of the mass media, together with Chávez's apparent apology for his own behaviour, served to persuade the right-wing opposition that their campaign could continue. They were helped by outside forces too; the right-wing governments of Chile and Colombia had given their support to the coup and Washington was now actively hostile to Chávez. It was significant that Cisneros had met with Bush's Latin American adviser, the notorious Otto Reich, during the coup preparations, for example. And while Chávez moved cautiously on the media, forming an investigating commission, the media moguls were mobilising their international networks (like the Interamerican Press Association) to denounce the Chávez government for its restrictions of freedom of expression. Anyone who has visited Venezuela will testify to the anarchy that prevails in the communications sector, and to the openly reactionary and personally abusive material broadcast daily on the private media. Yet the international campaign has managed to embed an image of a crazed dictator prohibiting any form of critical expression – a dangerous caricature. Some restrictions were imposed on broadcasters, but these tended to be placed on pro-Chávez media; these largely community-based broadcasters were increasingly popular, but they did not have the high production values the television audience was accustomed to. Nonetheless they had played a key role in mobilising against the coup and would do so again in the events later in the year.

It was clear by August that Chávez would not retaliate for the coup, and the right continued to direct its fire against Chávez personally. By August its activities began to accelerate. An uneasy alliance of conservative organisations, some elements of the left (Bandera Roja)[3] and business and trade union leaders, had formed the Democratic Coordinating Committee before the coup. It now began to organise again, focusing its activities on the overthrow of Chávez – the one demand that could unite this band of hostile brothers. The 1999 Constitution, ironically enough, had removed a clause criminalising any propaganda which encouraged people to disobey the law; Chávez replaced it with a call to repudiate bad laws. Thus Cecilio Sosa, a Supreme Court justice, could call on Venezuelans to disobey the law with impunity – starting with the obligation to pay income tax. And the CTV now felt able to publicly challenge the government again, though they were helped by the decision earlier in the year to cut social security and by the rising cost of living – fed by a deliberate strategy of creating shortages and arbitrarily increasing prices which the powerful private interests that dominated the food distribution industry pursued (and continue to pursue). The effect was not only to raise their profits arbitrarily but also to create an atmosphere of uncertainty and anxiety which was then reinforced and exacerbated by the hysterical media coverage.

Chávez himself was adopting a position which must have generated increasing confusion among his most ardent supporters. When the right wing announced its latest mobilisations in August, he wished them luck and promised that security forces would act with restraint. It may have been ironic, but it presented him as an arbiter between social forces rather than as the leader of the movement of the masses. And the opposition, in its turn, exploited that confusion for its own purposes. The call for a 'civic strike' in December was simply the second chapter of the campaign to remove Chávez. A twelve-hour protest in October was clearly a test. It failed to mobilise any significant numbers, but the social tensions were rising. In November the government intervened in the Metropolitan Police, still controlled by the opposition mayor Alfredo Peña, after a shootout between pro- and anti-Chávez officers which left two dead. The Commissioner Henry Vivas, still in post despite his active role in the April events, was now dismissed. Peña then refused to recognise his replacement – an open invitation to mutiny. Some days later, a group of army officers dismissed for their involvement in April appeared in the Plaza Altamira, the emblematic centre of Caracas's wealthy eastern area, and announced a permanent occupation 'until Chávez was overthrown'. In fact the protest eventually petered out, but it contributed to the atmosphere of permanent tension in the country. These and many other similar actions proved to be a prologue to the 2 December. On that day, a civic strike was announced again, coordinated by the executives of Pdvsa and supported by the trade union congress CTV and a range of other organisations.

The notion of a 'civic' strike suggested that it was a mobilisation of 'civil society', a concept that had gained currency in political discussions across the world. But the implication was that the participants were NGOs and other pressure groups and lobbying organisations independent of political parties and institutions. The reality, by contrast, was that this was a movement led and organised by elements of the old system, many of them still embedded in the Chavista state, including the old political parties and their new allies among those who had deserted the Chávez camp. Since its objective was clear the strike call was combined with a campaign to collect signatures for a referendum to recall Chávez, as the Constitution allowed. Under the Constitution, that could only take place at the mid-term point, in August 2003 at the earliest. The call for a February referendum, therefore, was a provocation and a means of organising physical opposition to the government, which was six months in advance of the permitted date.

By 3 December the strike seemed to be fading; many businesses had closed down, but many more had not. There were clashes in the streets, especially around Pdvsa offices, and the following day another huge right-wing demonstration marched on the city centre. This time, however, the object of the action that began on the 2nd was the oil industry, the life blood of the Venezuelan economy. The Pdvsa executives had acted in overtly political ways ever since Chávez was elected; now they would emerge as the leadership of the movement. They seemed very confident that their action would achieve its purposes in a matter of days. On the 4th the captain of the 'Pilin Leon' a massive oil tanker sailing through Lake Maracaibo, stopped its progress and announced that he had joined the strike. It was a declaration of war. The drifting tanker could have crashed into the huge Rafael Urdaneta bridge across the lake – causing incalculable damage to the bridge itself and the surrounding populated areas. It would also block the shipping lanes. But this was not a single act but part of a coordinated opposition strategy. On the 2nd, 18,000 staff had walked out of Pdvsa's offices and installations. It emerged subsequently that they had cut cables, deliberately damaged equipment and sabotaged installations. They then picketed offices, refineries and distribution depots to intimidate workers who had not joined the strike. There were even snipers on the roofs of buildings around Pdvsa offices, to intimidate those who elected to continue to work. Tankers could no longer reach petrol stations and the effects were immediate. Enormous queues formed in the hope that new gas and petrol supplies would arrive.

The true seriousness of the action did not emerge for some days. But on the 9th, Alí Rodríguez Araque, now president of Pdvsa, went on television to demand that staff return to work – since this was not an official strike – and more importantly, that they return computers and passwords without which an industry as highly technologised as this could not function. It then emerged that the IT running the industry had been out-sourced by the Pdvsa management to a company called Intesa. It was owned by SAIC, a US-based company linked to the US defence industry.[4] The strikers refused to provide that information. The consequences could be drastic. Safety meters on holding tanks would no longer function, the oil distribution network would be disrupted, the financial system collapse, gas and oil refineries would cease to function. And like a floating oil tanker, an uncontrollable oil refinery could quickly and easily become a time bomb. It was the ferocity and cynicism of this assault on the industry that gave the strikers and their leaders the confidence to assume that Chávez would lose control of the situation in a matter of days, his supporters would then turn against him, and he would be forced to resign – making the recall referendum unnecessary.

The anchored and sabotaged *Pilin Leon* in the waters of Lake Maracaibo symbolised the destructive intent of the opposition. Chávez sent soldiers to take over the ship but the crew (wisely) refused to leave it in the hands of unqualified people. Chávez withdrew the threat. And when a retired tanker captain, Carlos López, volunteered on 19 December to turn the ship around (an extremely complex exercise), López was escorted by local populations around the lake, and the National Guard, who ushered him through the barricades the strikers had put up to try and block his access. Such barricades were a feature of the strike – blockading access to installations and refineries, for instance, or halting traffic on highways. And it continued to be a favoured method for the right-wing opposition. Wherever workers loyal to the government attempted to keep production going, aggressive pickets were trying to intimidate them. More serious was the refusal of the holders of computer codes and passwords to return them. It was the skill of a group of young university hackers that restored them. The right, it seemed, had forgotten the slogan that emerged early in the Chávez era 'hungry or jobless, I'm sticking with Chávez' (*con hambre o sin empleo / con Chávez me resteo*). The mass movement once again mounted its collective resistance, on two levels. It actively fought the actions of the right, and it bore the grim consequences of its support for Chávez – queues, shortages, hunger, lack of services.

The damage caused by the bosses strike, as it is usually called, was enormous nonetheless. The opposition had demonstrated that it was prepared to destroy the economy in order to bring down Chávez. On 6 December the 'liberated' Altamira Square was packed and closed by the opposition-led police for a mass rally. In the early evening a Portuguese taxi driver opened fire, apparently indiscriminately, killing a young woman and injuring a number of others. He was immediately denounced as a Chavista, although he made no attempt to escape and never disclosed his reasons for the shooting. It was a crude and cynical attempt to repeat the actions at Puente Llaguno on 11 April, and provide a pretext for the opposition leaders to declare the strike indefinite.

By the beginning of the second week, shortages were starting to bite; food supplies were affected and the ATMs stopped giving out cash. A number of judges walked out. It was Christmas, the heaviest shopping season, yet many stores were closed. There were daily marches and *cacerolazos*, the banging of pots, a method of protest the opposition to Chávez had learned from the Chilean right-wing opposition to Allende in Chile. By the 13th Chávez did the unthinkable – he imported oil from neighbouring Latin American countries, and defaulted on his US customers. In mid-December the average daily production of around three million barrels was down to 150,000. It was no more than a trickle.

If Chávez had exhibited nervous hesitations in the aftermath of the April coup, his oversight of the defence of Pdvsa and the oil industry was firm and charismatic. This was a critical moment. It was an opportunity to face down and challenge the opposition, and mobilise his forces with the same single-mindedness as the right wing were mobilising theirs. Confronting a rabid media campaign and an opposition prepared to destroy the national economy, he responded with determination and clarity. It was as if he was at his best in those emergency situations in which improvised and spontaneous responses were the most appropriate. When Captain López successfully completed the dangerous manoeuvre of turning the monstrous structure *Pilin Leon* under the Maracaibo bridge, Chávez flew to join him on the bridge and thanked him on television.

The final days of 2003 were still extremely tense and difficult. An increasingly desperate opposition called on people to refuse to pay their taxes, but unlike their other actions, this was specifically forbidden under the Constitution. The Christmas/New Year period is a time for continuous partying in Venezuela, and shopping becomes the primary national sport. But not this time. There were severe shortages of the cooking gas that most poor people used and long queues formed for days where petrol stations were expecting new supplies. There *were* protest demonstrations – but they were directed at the people responsible for the shortages – the right. In mid-January, Carlos Ortega of the CTV still blustered that they were going to march on Miraflores; but the reality was that the strike was breaking down everywhere except in the oil industry. The Chavista march on 23 January, the anniversary of Pérez Jiménez's overthrow, was huge. The middle class spent the day behind their security fences, arms in hand, expecting the worst. But nothing happened. Within days the Caracas Stock Exchange reluctantly opened its doors and oil production passed the one million barrels a day mark. It had never actually ceased, but in December production had slowed to a trickle, so this was a highly symbolic milestone.

The damage to the economy was already enormous. Yet the opposition was still bent on its destructive course. The conduct of the media was unparalleled; commercial advertising was suspended and their spots filled with relentless calls to overthrow the government. Every day at 6 p.m. the leaders of the bosses strike gave a press conference which was broadcast simultaneously by every channel. And while it was true that their fire was concentrated on the figure of Chávez, their purpose was to bring down the whole Bolivarian project.

The process was unprecedented in the history of Venezuela. Although there had been few significant changes in their material conditions (although education was now free and there was greater access to health) for a wide spectrum of the popular sectors this was their government. The right saw this as a serious threat to their positions as the masters of the country. That is why it was not just a matter now of getting rid of Chávez but of bringing down the project and destroying the forces of change, to achieve a new liberal constitution, and to force those popular sectors to return to their role as the resigned and excluded poor.[5]

In early March, the strike finally collapsed. That their project failed so badly is testimony to the tenacity of the majority of Venezuelans, who once again discovered their capacity to organise their own resistance and their own survival. For Chávez, the end of the strike in March was a major victory and he revelled in it. But on reflection it exposed some serious problems for the future. No collective political leadership of the Chavista process had emerged in the course of the strike; most of the ministers were invisible and, with the exception of Alí Rodríguez, Chávez seemed to be taking all the day to day decisions. The opposition leadership gave daily bulletins in the name of the Coordinadora Democrática. Chávez spoke for himself. In fact he had very few communications media at his disposal, in contrast to the opposition, and it could be argued that his most powerful weapon was Radio Bemba (word of mouth), the organisations of workers in the oil industry, and the independent grassroots media.

This was both a strength and a weakness. In the absence of any form of organised relationship between Chávez and his base in the movement, it was his personal reputation, his charisma and his eloquence that sustained it. In the crisis of the bosses strike he had shown the greatest determination and strength; but he had placed himself even more firmly at the centre of the Bolivarian revolution. Yet the events the country had just lived through demonstrated very clearly not just where the real forces for change were to be found, but also how far they had come in terms both of consciousness and organisation. For the second time in a year, the people had ensured the revolution's survival. Chávez himself, in a speech on 10 February, had drawn the logic of the times, quoting Bolívar's advice: 'If you want to end poverty give power to the poor.'[6]

It seemed that he was ready to follow through the logic of power from below.

A Mission to Transform

There were surprisingly few reprisals in the aftermath of this frontal assault on the Bolivarian revolution. But the 18,000 Pdvsa employees – personnel managers, executives, technicians, half the workforce who had broken their contract (a strike was never officially declared) – were dismissed. The February recall referendum which the opposition had called for as part of its overall strategy, was postponed, since Chávez had not yet reached his mid-term in August 2003. It did eventually take place, a year later. The opposition managed to gather the required number of signatures, though the campaign was intense and conflictive, with the opposition crying fraud throughout, denouncing the National Electoral Commission, and reviving their accusations of Cuban influence and covert communism. The situation was made more complex because the procedures for a recall had not yet been worked out, and evolved en route to the vote. Chávez campaigned with even more than his usual energy, encouraging voter registration and naturalising foreign residents, the bulk of them poor immigrants. In the event, and despite absurd opposition claims to the contrary, Chávez won 59 per cent of the votes in a poll in which 70 per cent of those eligible voted.

There are many ways of explaining the victory – manipulation, use of the media, falsification of results – put forward by an enraged right wing. The reality, however, is rather simpler; Chávez enjoyed mass support, which he encouraged very skilfully, albeit spending rather more on his campaigning than had been normal prior to that. The economic losses sustained as a result of the strike were enormous – some estimates suggest $11 billion. But beyond the actual amounts involved, far more damaging was the effect on the economy overall. In the first and second quarters of 2003, GDP fell by 15 per cent and 25 per cent respectively. Oil production, normally around three million barrels a day, fell to its lowest point to 150,000, paralysing the economy. Hundreds of small and medium businesses went to the wall. By the end of 2004, however, the price of oil was at $40, reaching $57 by the end of the following year. Although Pdvsa was Latin America's largest company, it came around 50th on the scale of efficiency. Now its profits would return to the state and any private companies involved would pay a high level of royalties – at least 30 per cent. Thus, despite the crisis of 2003, Chávez was able to announce the creation of the Missions, the social programmes promised in the 1999 Constitution, and financed by oil revenues, which had barely begun to be set in motion until then. They could be seen as a reward for the selfless support of the majority of the country during the bosses strike, their patient acceptance of real sacrifices in defence of Chávez and his government.

The new Pdvsa 'now embarked on an impressive campaign of corporate responsibility and social charity',[7] financing a series of social programmes. Impressive it certainly was. There were 24 Social Missions, focusing on health, education, housing as well as indigenous rights, voter registration and others. While many Venezuelans had enjoyed some of the fruits of oil in the 1970s, particularly in education, neo-liberal adjustment programmes had driven over 60 per cent of the population into poverty (and half of those into extreme poverty) by the late 1990s. Education had in effect been privatised (if not formally), and health provision was largely limited to the private sector, to which the majority of Venezuela's poor and working class were denied access. A glimpse around Caracas's hillside barrios was enough to indicate how serious the housing problem was.

The higher levels of public spending during the oil boom of the 1970s were clearly not part of any radical proposal, but rather the expression of a paternalistic relationship between the state and the people. They were gifts of the state in exchange for acquiescence or support. The living standards of the majority of Venezuelans had plummeted in the wake of the austerity measures taken by Carlos Andrés Pérez, and the poorest were the worst affected. It was critical to Chávez's promise of a new and different Venezuela that the cuts were restored. The phrase used in the Information document, however, is telling – 'social charity' indicates the same paternalistic attitude (though it may simply be a bad translation) and points to the phenomenon known as *asistencialismo*, the provision of services by the state as an act of charity. But this is very different from the provision of services as a right, as part of the social wage, paid for by taxation (and potentially redistributing wealth across the whole society). The Misiones were set in motion with characteristic ambiguities. On the one hand they were seen as Chávez's gesture of thanks and as a kind of reward, paid for out of oil revenues which were, in practice, a presidential fund administered directly rather than via the ministries. On the other hand, they were represented as institutions of a new order, administered from the grassroots by the service users – in other words, as manifestations of a participatory democracy.

Nevertheless, the improvements were visible, particularly in education and health. Chávez was deeply committed to education, logically enough since he had been a beneficiary of a higher education which permitted social mobility to many of his background. And his conception of a democracy involved an informed and educated population. By 2001, 770,000 people had moved into higher education (through the Misión Sucre), others were able to complete their high school courses (Misión Ribas) and Misión Robinson (a reference to Simón Rodríguez, who had adopted that name) attacked illiteracy. By 2001, Venezuela's illiteracy rate was below 6.4 per cent. A new university, the Bolivariana, was announced by Chávez on his Sunday morning *Aló Presidente* programme in mid 2003. Characteristically, he had informed none of those involved that Pdvsa had ceded an old office building in the city centre which would now become the Bolivarian University. I spoke to the administrators who were charged with setting up the admissions process – with no entry criteria, no furniture and no notion of numbers. They had two weeks to prepare. Their panic was mixed with a kind of civic pride, as they described the sleepless nights they had before they opened. Thirty-three thousand applicants arrived to take advantage of the opportunity in its first year. The levels of educational involvement would certainly continue to improve with the establishment of the Misiones, but Venezuela had experienced high levels of social spending previously, though it fell dramatically in the 1990s. In Latin American terms, therefore, Venezuela was quite high on the scale of public spending. The point, however, was not just the level of investment in these sectors, which certainly fell as neo-liberalism tightened its grip, but also the politics of that investment.[8]

One and a half million joined the two stages of the Misión Robinson and the Bolivarian University's first intake was around 20,000 of the 33,000 applicants. Furthermore the University Villages took the university to the more remote communities. The agreements with Cuba in 2000 guaranteed the provision of oil in exchange for medical and other technical personnel (teachers, sports instructors etc.). The Barrio Adentro (Into the Barrios) Mission was the most emblematic. Venezuelan doctors were indisputably members of the upper-middle class and worked for the most part in the private sector; unsurprisingly they overwhelmingly supported the opposition and essentially abandoned the public health system when Chávez came to power. To fill that gap, and provide care to Venezuela's poor, 13,000 Cuban doctors went to Venezuela to work in the scheme. The service was efficient, if basic, and later developed diagnostic and specialist centres. At the same time, a new generation of students of medicine began their studies in Cuba and later at the Bolivarian University – most were unconditionally pro-Chávez. Food distribution was also addressed through the popular supermarkets, Mercal, which offered basic provisions at knockdown prices. This was particularly important because the right wing used shortages of goods as a weapon, just as they had in Chile in 1972–73.

In a speech on 12 November 2004, Chávez reviewed the reasons for the creation of the Missions:

You'll remember that because of the coup and the damage it caused, the country became increasingly ungovernable, because of the economic crisis, our own errors, and there was a moment when we were no better, or even worse off than before. There was a survey a friend recommended to me and then he said something that hit me hard: 'President, if there was a referendum now you'd lose' ... That's when we began to work on the Missions; we designed it and then we went to Fidel for help ... Hundreds of medics started to arrive, planes coming and going all the time, improving the economy, organising the barrios. And we created the Missions ... and then, well, we began to go up in the polls, and they're never wrong. It's not magic, it's politics, and look where we are now.[9]

In terms of Chávez's political manifesto, the Missions were clearly a flagship programme. But as his speech shows, it was one born out of political necessity, and it was essentially improvised. The Missions were not part of a considered plan or a social welfare strategy, but a response to immediate circumstances. Thus while Barrio Adentro was visibly an improvement in the quality of life for Venezuela's poorest, it was uneven across the country and provided primary care at the expense of long-term hospital treatment. The state of the hospitals by the end of the decade, as Chávez himself recognised, was lamentable. In speeches earlier that year, Chávez had emphasised community participation and announced the creation of the *consejos comunales*, or community councils. In some sense, the success of the programme was counted in votes – and manifest in the high level of support in the recall referendum. But while the Bolivarian Circles had done their job well, there was no perceptible shift towards a different kind of social organisation. The state continued in its functions which were then mirrored in the Missions; this was inefficient and wasteful, and the confusion between the two served to veil the mismanagement and corruption that these programmes fostered. Since everything was done in response to immediate needs, the longer term objectives of the Missions remained unclear and their activities were rarely monitored, as the Contralor, a sort of state ombudsman, Clodovaldo Rusian, frequently complained.[10]

There was no doubting the achievements of the education programmes. By 2005 Venezuela was declared by Unesco to be free of illiteracy; school building increased from 2000 onwards, doubling the previous five-year figures. The numbers in higher education increased and by 2007 the Integrated Medicine programmes were producing a whole new generation of medical personnel. Mercal, again because of its essentially improvised character, began to have problems to do with hygiene and distribution mechanisms very early on, and the long queues at the markets and the manipulations of private concessionaires undermined the promise of access in conditions of dignity that had been promised.

For many on the left, the Missions appeared to offer the skeleton of a different kind of state, led by the organised people, its strategies

Figure 6.1   Chávez during the literacy campaign –
the Misión Robinson

a response to their demands. Perhaps this was the embryo of a
participatory democracy that went far beyond representation to
direct control? That was the tantalising possibility, and there was
certainly a sense of vigorous and committed involvement as the
Missions got under way. The state institutions were still largely
dominated by the old functionaries and there was a mounting anger
at what was seen as a combination of sabotage (a general go-slow)
and the continuing corruption of the system. The leadership of
the Missions were a new layer, generally younger and from poorer
backgrounds; many were sent to Cuba for training courses, practical
and ideological. The problem was that the two systems worked in
parallel but not in any coordinated way – in fact, as the health sector
showed, they would often compete. But in neither area was there any
sense of strategic planning. It was perhaps in housing where this was

most obvious, where there was a consistent failure to reach housing targets throughout the Chávez years.

Nonetheless, in terms of aspirations the period 2004–06 seems to be the most radical moment in the Bolivarian revolution. Michael Albert certainly felt that to be the case when he visited Venezuela. The officials he spoke to (and he seems to have spoken mainly to officials) were enthusiastic about the communal councils and the Mission. 'There is no need, however, the officials said, to remove or otherwise forcefully conflict with the old structures. Rather, the new system would be built alongside what now exists and would prove its worth in time, in parallel.'[11] Yet, as we have seen in the case of health, that meant distorting the pattern of investment in hospitals and operating without a clear strategic plan. The same applied to other sectors. More importantly, it ignored a reality that had revealed itself time and again. The old bureaucracy remained in place and was aggressive in its systematic and deliberate sabotage of every government initiative. Yet it was left to itself to continue its subversions.

Hugo Chávez had a vision of his own, but while it appeared to be based on the creation of alternative organs of power – *poder popular* – the old structures remained in place, and rather than the new parallel power gradually undermining the old state, the reverse was true, and increasingly so. The central cause was the fact that while Chavismo had taken a significant part of political power, it had no strategy for taking control of the economy beyond the oil sector. It might be argued that that was enough, given its dominance. But the problem as Gregory Wilpert pointed out, was 'the Dutch disease', namely the fact that there was no expansion of production in any other sector; instead, industrial and consumer goods were imported using oil revenues.

The income from oil financed the Missions and the range of social programmes, but none of these represented a long-term investment in expanding domestic production. To do that might have meant cutting back on some areas of public spending in the short term, with an eye on the future. But in a perspective that, increasingly made decisions in response to imminent elections and short term advantage, that kind of planning was repeatedly set aside. There was nothing to say that Chávez had to be an economist of course; and he had advisers to help him address these issues. But they too depended on Chávez's pleasure and as Chávez himself said in the November 2004 speech, very few people dared to criticise him. In a more collective leadership there would be a range of opinions and analyses to compare and debate in the light of a longer-term perspective. But Chávez had become even more sceptical of party organisation, and there were certainly no credible organisations in Venezuela to serve as a reference point.

Once again, the sense is of unresolved contradictions. The Missions could have provided the basis for a different political organisation, a network of democratic organs of control. Instead they were conduits of state policy but not participants in its development. But there were some signs of new directions. Towards the end of 2004, Chávez had begun to speak of 'cogestión', a form of workers self-management in conjunction with the state; here he was advised by Carlos Lanz, the Marxist ex-guerrilla, who had a developed strategy for implementing and developing workers control. But he was emphatic that this was not the kind of co-management that had been tried in Europe. This was 'revolutionary co-management', direct democracy in the workplace and a logical extension of the Constitution's emphasis on participatory democracy.[12] The model for this new form was to be Alcasa, the aluminium production plant where Lanz was appointed director early in 2005. The role of workers in the revolution had rarely been addressed, and on a number of occasions Chávez exhibited a degree of scepticism about trade union organisation. This was possibly understandable against the background of a trade union movement controlled by a corrupt CTV which had never represented workers' real interests. The emergence of the UNT, a new rank-and-file union federation, at around this time, created the possibility of genuinely independent trade union organisation with elected leaders and consistent workplace organisation. But it soon clashed with Chávez's Ministry of Labour, dominated by his appointees, and with the Bolivarian Federation of Labour (FBT) which was a seedbed for a new but equally unaccountable trade union bureaucracy. UNT's first congress was severely disrupted by internal conflicts and soon split between political currents. But it remained the case that Chávez had expressed no views about the role of workers in the *proceso*.

Porto Alegre: Twenty-First-Century Socialism

January 2005 marked a new phase in the revolution, and a moment at which Hugo Chávez seized the attention of anti-capitalists across the world. The World Social Forum was meeting in Porto Alegre, Brazil. The opening rally had been addressed by Lula, elected a year earlier to the presidency of Brazil. His humble background, not unlike Chávez's, and his role as a workers' leader and a founder member of the Workers Party (PT) led many to anticipate that his presidency would address the significant social privations in Brazil and the difficulties faced by trade unionists. Instead he presented a programme which was neo-liberal in its content, with some elements of welfare directed at the poor (like Fome Zero). Thus his arrival in Porto Alegre was not greeted with universal applause – in the stadium he was heckled by some of the participants in the Forum. At the end of the week Hugo Chávez arrived to speak in the same stadium. But before travelling to the stadium he had gone to a land occupation organised by Brazil's Landless People's Movement (MST), an organisation which had expressed extreme disappointment with Lula. When he arrived in the stadium he was received in ways normally reserved for media stars, and instantly won over the 15,000 in his audience with his ease of communication and his ebullient charm. Then, to the delight of those listening, he announced that Venezuela was embarking on the road of twenty-first-century socialism.

Chávez had never used the term socialism before, though he had frequently referred to Marx, Gramsci and other Marxists in his speeches. His performance at Porto Alegre was masterly. For one and a half hours he combined wit, personal comments and denunciations of imperialism with the customary references to Bolívar. In a key passage, he said, to roars of approval, that we have to go beyond capitalism towards a socialism of justice and equality. But, he added, this 'could be done in a democracy'.

The Porto Alegre speech illustrated very clearly the paradoxes of Chávez's position, and the difficulty of locating him within one or other political tradition. He reminds his audience of the significance of the Bandung Conference, he refers to Marx and Engels and acknowledges that Che Guevara's vision of the revolutionary transition is no longer viable. And he devotes some time to China, whose economic miracle he praises. He even describes himself as a youthful Maoist (though there is very little evidence for that).

Chávez's speech at Porto Alegre resonated around the world. He was, it seemed, reclaiming a socialist tradition that had fallen into discredit with many of the social movements since the fall of the Berlin Wall. Yet his practice suggested an idea of socialism closer to social democracy than the revolutionary project of Marx or Lenin. In Venezuela, private capital co-existed with Chavismo, its conflicts restricted to the arena of politics. Chávez had signed new operating agreements for oil exploration in the Orinoco with several foreign firms in the previous years. Pdvsa retained a 51 per cent investment, but the arrangements were extremely favourable to the minority partners.

The reference to China and Iran in the speech were extremely significant; for most socialists around the world neither regime could lay claim to the Marxist inheritance. And nor indeed could Russia (Chávez described Putin as a good man), or Gaddafi (who was also approvingly mentioned in the speech), or Lula (for whom Chávez reserved his final assurances of friendship). These were allies in a third-world perspective, the essential theme of his speech, when he spoke of the 'resurgence of the South'. In his relations with the rest of Latin America, Chávez was a more consistent Bolivarian in his pursuit of regional integration. But for the rest, the international policy of the Bolivarian revolution pointed inexorably towards the creation of a new third-world bloc for the global age.

The problem is that if economic relationships are determined only by mutual interests, how can that be distinguished from political relationships? If, for example, Venezuela was a defender of human rights on the international stage, as Chávez so often insisted it was, then how could that be reconciled with silence in the face of China's well-attested abuses of human rights? Vladimir Putin had overseen a concentration of wealth and power in the hands of a new economic oligarchy, warring among themselves but now operating as one more actor in the global market. How could that be justified in the radical democratic terms to which Chávez made reference in his Porto Alegre speech? The answer, presumably, was the same argument put forward by Fidel on various occasions – political survival in a hostile world. Venezuela, however, is dependent on oil production which locates it centrally in the global system; and national economic growth is clearly envisaged as the result of an exchange between national capitals based exclusively on the law of value. Beside it, however, is a concept of a fraternal and egalitarian integration of equal exchange between Latin American nations enshrined in ALBA (the Bolivarian Alternative for Latin America). For this was Chávez's alternative to the Free Trade Area of the Americas and the other regional organisations whose objective would be to tie the region more securely to the global market. It could and did produce some wonderful examples of solidarity and visionary thinking – in educational exchange, in the unity of indigenous peoples, in the exchange of radical ideas. Yet these nations were themselves dependent on a world market and the multinational corporations that prevailed there.

If it is true that survival in the harsh conditions of a world economy dominated by neo-liberalism is a daily challenge, the task of socialists is to develop the possibilities for building a new and different system, strengthening the capacity for independent organisation of the majority populations whose exploitation and alienation is the driving force of that system. A state dedicated to capital accumulation in this way cannot at one and the same time devolve power to the grassroots and advance the system of exploitation. It is an insoluble paradox.

In 2005 Chávez travelled widely – his tally of countries visited had now passed 130. He had also moved to consolidate his own control over the state. His first objective was control of the media with a new media law and the creation of a new Latin American television channel Telesur, run by Andrés Izarra, previously his Communications minister. In March 2005, Chávez met with leaders of the 'new left' governments of Latin America. It presaged the extension of ALBA and a further step towards the Bolivarian dream of Latin American integration. But Venezuela's generosity towards other Latin American nations did not meet with the approval of all Venezuelans. It was not simply a kind of collective egotism that was involved, but the recognition by many Venezuelans that the transformations they had expected and hoped for were very slow in coming. In September that year, Chávez again visited the United Nations and won himself at least half the world's applause when he made his famous remark about the smell of sulphur when he followed Bush to the speaker's podium. His anti-imperialist discourse was growing more intense, and it was of a piece with a policy of Latin American integration uniting the region in a shared distrust of Washington. His reputation was further enhanced when, in contrast to the indifference of the Bush administration, Chávez offered help to the victims of Hurricane Katrina in New Orleans, in the form of cheap fuel oil.

2006 was a good year for everyone. The land laws and the new Misión Guaicaipuro, returning indigenous lands to their communities, promised a new stage in the revolution. The banking and the financial sectors had a good year too; profits were up in those sectors and in the commercial arena. Yet the beneficiaries of those increased profit rates were private capitalists, many working in conjunction with multinational collaborators.[13] And most importantly, while the rising price of oil was allowing increased levels of consumption, there was little sign of diversification in the economy or increased production outside the oil industry. And the much-vaunted commitment to social production, the expansion of cooperatives and workers control seemed to be progressing at a snail's pace. The two iconic examples of co-management, Alcasa and the paper factory Venapal, were forms of workers management, but they had neither been expropriated nor nationalised. Chávez's economic policies were in Richard Gott's words 'little more than a moderate social democratic programme'[14] or 'gradual reform';[15] yet his political message remained radical and democratic. Clearly what Chávez meant by socialism was a transformation of culture, educational levels, and a more democratic political system. But he did not follow the Marxist tradition in understanding socialism to be above all a transformation of social *and* productive relations.

Far from becoming more transparent and democratic, Chávez's absolutely central role in the process was making that far more unlikely. In the 2004 regional and municipal elections, as he proudly reminded his Porto Alegre audience, Chavismo had won 21 out of 23 governorships and 80 per cent of the country's mayoralties. More significantly, the landslide had brought into office a range of candidates with no real roots in their areas and even less experience – candidates who had been chosen *a dedo*, as the Spanish has it, in other words at the will and caprice of the president, and who were therefore dependent for their political survival on him. It was a formula for corruption and the creation of a layer of loyal and unquestioning political functionaries who were extremely unlikely to debate presidential decisions or criticise errors. Especially since a new presidential election was imminent, in December 2006.

6

The Contradictions of Twenty-first-century Socialism

ugo Chávez won the 2006 elections with a 63 per cent majority, the largest so far. The campaign had been long and relentless – and its costs had been very high. Telesur and the state TV channel ran series of advertisements proclaiming the successes of Chavismo, which focused overwhelmingly on Chávez himself. His travels and his passionate pursuit of integration, expressed through ALBA, led him to a number of countries, where he was faithfully followed in press and media. He was now projected on to an international stage as a world statesman. Despite the increasingly presidentialist message, however, it was also true that there were other reasons that explained the strength of his support. He was still riding on his successful battle against the opposition in 2002–03 and 2004, which had left it disorientated and with no credible candidate to rival Chávez. The fact that Manuel Rosales, governor of Zulia province, had emerged as the presidential candidate of the right, despite his murky financial past, was evidence that the old AD bureaucrats were again reasserting themselves, and that the opposition had nothing new to offer. In fact his candidacy probably garnered a number of votes for Chávez. The Missions, heavily criticised from the right though they were, had brought real material improvements in people's lives, particularly in education, where the achievement was most visible, and health, where the now familiar hexagonal medical centres of Barrio Adentro were emerging everywhere, though their number still fell far short of the promised 9,500. Poverty was down from 44 per cent to 38 per cent of the population. In housing, perhaps the most intractable of social problems, the targets were rarely reached and towards the end of the decade the Housing Ministry would acknowledge the crisis, although the colourful Petrocasas built by Pdvsa were visible across the country.

In January 2007, some firms were nationalised, with compensation at market prices, including the telephone company Cantv. The troublesome television channel, Radio Caracas TV (RCTV), always a bastion of the right, was refused a new licence for terrestrial broadcasts. This provoked demonstrations and protests within Venezuela, predominantly by students, who were re-emerging as the public face of the opposition, and outside the country, in the US and Spain, for example, where the decision was described as a new attack on freedom of expression. In fact RCTV had not paid its taxes for years, and in any event continued to broadcast, with its characteristic anti-Chávez bile, on cable.

Immediately after the election, Chávez announced the allocation of $18 billion for the Community Councils (*consejos comunales*) which had been promised but not yet allocated. The councils had come to be seen as the embodiment of the promised participatory democracy. And yet, despite Chávez's announcement, their implementation would once again be delayed and their role remained ambiguous. And there were other developments that seemed to point in a different direction. Pdvsa, for example, now had a new president, replacing Alí Rodríguez Araque. Rafael Ramírez had a far left past, and his father had been a guerrilla fighter, yet his arrival at Pdvsa brought with it a change in management structures as well as a new face. In the two years after the bosses strike, there had been a serious move to run the corporation in a collective and democratic way, through direct workers involvement in assemblies at which the executives argued for their strategies. With Ramírez, the corporation returned to a hierarchical form of organisation in which the executives acted without consultation with the workforce and solely in conjunction with the Minister of Energy – coincidentally Ramírez himself – in direct consultation with Chávez. It was one sign of the concentration of power in the state machine in a new bureaucracy.

The PSUV: A Cuban Model?

Immediately after the election, Chávez announced the formation of a new party – the United Socialist Party of Venezuela (PSUV).

Its formation, and the characteristically improvised way in which it was sprung on the nation, caused enormous controversy. A mass ruling party that simply arises out of the will of a leader cannot claim to be organic to the revolutionary process, nor the product of democratic decision making. It was declared, not discussed. But with the enormous authority of a recently re-elected Hugo Chávez behind it, it was hard to resist. In effect, it undermined every other existing political organisation in one dramatic gesture. The president who had built his reputation on a rejection of *partidocracia* – the rule of the party – had now formed, overnight, a party as an instrument of state power. The implications were far-reaching. A party that had not grown organically out of the movement could not claim to be democratic in the Marxist sense of an instrument for self-emancipation. There had been no opportunity to discuss its structures or its objectives. They were simply announced and people invited to support them. It was defended, of course, with two kinds of argument – one that Chavismo was the movement, and Chávez its incarnation, the other that it would become democratic, once formed, by virtue of a vigorous internal life. The first argument, in any of its many varieties, served the purposes of a bureaucracy that elided party and state functions and which laid claim to speak with the voice or the approval of Chávez. The second proved very quickly to be a cynical evasion. Within weeks a second announcement was made that the structures and policies would be decided respectively by two four man (and they were men) commissions nominated by the president. Their conclusions would then be voted on – not criticised or commented upon – by the nearly six million Venezuelans who had answered Chávez's call.

For the left the call posed an insoluble dilemma. If they wanted to continue to have a relationship with the poor and the working class, who were overwhelmingly (but not exclusively) those who had joined the new party, then they would have to be within its structures. Beyond the margins of the party lay isolation and marginality and ultimately irrelevance, inside a political culture of obedience and loyalty. Promises were made of transparency and freedom of internal debate, of course. But the reality was of control from above and of a vigilant internal bureaucracy that stamped down hard on internal dissent.

The PSUV did not correspond to any of the traditional models available from Venezuelan history, though some suggested that it was in fact a machinery of patronage like, for example, the Mexican PRI or indeed Venezuela's own Acción Democrática. To even raise a doubt about PSUV's democratic credentials was to be immediately labelled *escuálido*, Chávez's picturesque word for the opposition, in the endless war of words that was the daily substitute for serious political discussion. So what were its origins, if not in Venezuela's own past?

It is my view that the answer is – in Cuba. Cuban influence, always significant given Chávez's unswerving admiration for Fidel Castro, had grown exponentially since Chávez's arrival in power. Castro had negotiated oil deals with Carlos Andrés Pérez in the 1980s, and his concern for Pérez's welfare during the Caracazo was well known. But Chávez had cemented his relationship with Cuba in the period after his release from prison. In 1994, Caldera invited the leader of the anti-Castro lobby in the US, Jorge Mas Canosa, to visit Venezuela. In a typically subtle gesture, Castro responded by inviting Chávez to visit Cuba – and ostentatiously welcoming him personally at Havana airport. Ever since then, the two men had cultivated a close relationship in which Castro was the father-figure and mentor to the younger man. It was rare for Chávez to fail to mention Fidel in his public utterances, as if Fidel's seal of approval were the final guarantee of revolutionary validity. In 2000, Venezuela and Cuba signed the first of a series of agreements, which included the guaranteed provision of 53,000 barrels of oil per day at discount prices. In exchange for that, Cuba would provide medical and technical personnel, and open its medical school to young Venezuelan students, as well as treat patients there with major surgical needs.

For Cuba, there can be little doubt that this was a godsend; it was only just emerging from the 'special period in time of peace' that had wreaked such havoc after the collapse of the Soviet bloc.[1] The Cuban personnel in Venezuela were also paid in dollars, which had a double effect – of introducing scarce dollars into the Cuban economy, but also of creating a privileged layer with newly acquired patterns of consumption. Though it is rarely discussed, Cuban intelligence and military personnel were brought into Venezuela's state agencies in the wake of the April coup and the 2002–03 bosses strike. Cuba's support through the bosses strike was also rewarded with new agreements in 2004 and 2005, increasing the amount of oil sent to Cuba to 90,000 barrels and raising the number of grant-supported Venezuelan students in Cuba (a kind of veiled subsidy). Those sent to Cuba were not only sent to study for degrees in medicine and technical subjects – they were also sent for training, practical and ideological. Thus the newly launched Misión Robinson employed the Cuban method *Yo sí puedo*. Misión Barrio Adentro now included some 17,000 Cuban doctors and dentists, and the new sports organisations were predominantly run by Cuban advisers. And as the ALBA project gained momentum, Cuba's support was immensely significant in political terms, as well as extending its medical and educational contribution to other ALBA nations. Chávez was a regular visitor to Cuba; when Castro fell from a speaking platform and was injured, Chávez diverted his aircraft to visit him. And much of the last period of his life was, of course, spent in Cuba benefitting from its strength in medicine.

The relationship between the two leaders grew closer as the decade unfolded. Yet in 2002, Castro had emphatically affirmed that Chávez had never used the word socialism in their discussions. And when he did begin to use the term, in his Porto Alegre speech, its meaning clearly was very different from the 'actually existing socialism' of Eastern Europe or Cuba itself, where even the most sympathetic observer could not claim that Cuba offered an example of the kind of participatory democracy that Chávez was advocating. On the contrary, the country was controlled by a bureaucratic elite working under the direct supervision of Fidel, even after he had renounced all his official posts. The ruling Cuban Communist Party was run from above and its procedures for debate and open election were minimal, independently of how rarely party congresses occurred. Yet the structures of Chávez's new party, the PSUV, mimicked almost exactly those of the Cuban Communist Party, and were equally hierarchical and centralised. Later, Castro would implicitly defend Chávez's general thesis on the transition by arguing, as in fact Raul was arguing from the pinnacle of the Cuban government, that socialism could be compatible with the market.

The coincidence of the creation of the communal councils with the launch of the PSUV could be seen as an attempt to create equivalent local organisations to Cuba's Committees for the Defence of the Revolution (CDRs), though the latter's functions, given the circumstances of their original creation at the time of the Bay of Pigs invasion in 1961, were principally those of vigilance and control. But they (and the *comunas* that were advocated in similar terms later) were presented as something very different, as a new stage in the development of popular participation and grassroots democracy. In fact, the meetings of the councils seemed principally to be concerned with local issues, and to be much more akin to forms of municipal government rather than having the overtly political and activist function of the Bolivarian Circles, for example, of two years earlier. Discussion in the *consejos* ranged around local problems and often focused on the corruption of local officials and their misuse of public funds. Yet any discussion of the global policy decisions made by Chávez was limited to praise and uncritical support.

The beneficiaries of that support were not the people themselves, who by and large continued to exhibit the extraordinary patience and fortitude they had shown time and again in their enthusiasm for Chávez, but the emerging new layer of bureaucrats. The loyalty of Chávez's supporters did not speak the truth to power, nor criticise nor argue. It was a loyalty that buried unpromising statistics and misrepresented what was actually being achieved as opposed to the declared objectives. As Luis Tascón put it: 'We carried out a profound transformation of political discourse; we changed the words, but not the practices.'[2]

Tascón was an extremely popular deputy in the National Assembly with a background on the far left and a record of complete integrity. His name was associated with a publication of the list of signatories to the recall referendum, the consequences of which was the preparation of a blacklist of people who would never find jobs in the Chavista sector, public or private, again. When he began to make public reference to the emerging new bureaucratic class which was feathering its own nest and reproducing the corruption and inefficiency of earlier times, he was bitterly criticised within Chavismo. His book length interview with Ramon Hernández added extensive detail to his devastating critique of Chavismo from within, for Tascón could certainly not be accused of belonging to the opposition. Referring to the successful campaign around the recall referendum, Tascón argues that their contribution in exposing the forgeries and signatures of the dead had made it possible to postpone the referendum for six months and ensure that it was held in more favourable conditions

> ... when the Missions were having their effect and we were going up in the polls. We did it well, but not everything was so good. While we were doing that there were people who were just becoming more powerful, doing business, founding banks and managing exchange controls for their own benefit. Diosdado Cabello and other groups devoted themselves to accumulating power while the rest of us were defending and strengthening the revolution. The process began to take the wrong road in 2004, and the groups in power began to exclude us. We revolutionaries were no longer needed.[3]

These views, of course, were extremely unpopular; but Tascón, and the small group around him were not. He was taken seriously, and in any event what he said corresponded to the experience of growing numbers of people.[4] In fact Gregory Wilpert,[5] who was much closer to the leadership than Tascón, had perceptively warned before the 2006 elections of the dangers inherent in seeing the Missions as a kind of parallel state, when the existing state, with all its real, legal powers, still existed under the domination of the right. Inevitably, Wilpert argued, there would be a pull in both directions and either the state would be pulled towards the Missions or the reverse would happen, and the leadership of the Missions would gradually be sucked into the existing state with all its seductions, corruptions, and material possibilities. By 2007, it was becoming clear that this was exactly what had happened, as powerful allies of Chávez began to build their own personal empires and to profit from their access to power.

But where was Chávez? Since he was well known for being on top of pretty much everything, especially now that the Cuban intelligence services were involved, he must surely have seen what was going on. There is no evidence that Chávez was in any way personally corrupt; his family however, had enriched themselves, and Chávez had a furious public row with one relative who was driving around in a Hummer, an adapted military vehicle which was a favourite and extremely dangerous plaything of the very rich. There was physical evidence of the misuse of public funds which became a favourite theme of public gossip; in the state of Miranda, for example, when Diosdado Cabello was its governor, a very long motorway access point stopped in mid air. And anyone driving into Caracas would notice the curious pyramidal structure on an island in the centre of the motorway at Kilometre o, for which there was no obvious purpose and to which, in any case, there was no access. Yet it was built at huge expense by a relative of Juan Barreto, at that point the mayor of Caracas. The trade in dollars and the dramatically rising import bill for food, technology and industrial products, was making some people very rich indeed – the very same families who had controlled so much of the economy before 1998 and were still doing so now. And these people – Cisneros, the Mendozas – appeared to have become reconciled with Chávez.

Tascón's argument, and it was echoed by others, was that Chávez had become 'a prisoner of power' – though whether he meant that he had been seduced by power or that he was besieged and manipulated by powerful people was not clear.

The test was whether the process was now moving into a phase of decentralising and giving some real power to the grassroots and community organisations like the community councils. At the level of rhetoric that was certainly what was supposed to happen. Yet the law on community councils made them subject to a national leadership appointed by Chávez, and their functions included 'social intelligence' – a delicate way of describing informing on your neighbours. It appeared that the Cuban CDR model was more relevant than had at first appeared to be the case. Thus 'people's power' (*poder popular*) seemed to be hamstrung from the outset, as environmental activist María Pilar García Guadilla suggested in a 2007 report:

While the stated objectives and the discourse of the president speak of empowerment, transformation and democratization, the practice points towards clientilism, co-optation and exclusion as a consequence of political polarization. Giving communities resources while they lack the expertise and the mechanisms to guarantee transparency makes them more vulnerable to clientilism, dependency and co-optation ... .[6]

In December 2007, the Venezuelan public faced yet another election. Certainly not even the most virulent opponent of Chávez could claim that Venezuelans were not given regular and frequent opportunities to vote. In this case, it was a vote on a package of Constitutional amendments that had been presented to the National Assembly by Chávez before presenting them to the country. The National Assembly rarely debated such matters in any depth, given its overwhelming Chavista majority. The proposal included three particularly controversial provisions: an administrative reorganisation of the country, the so-called New Geometry of Power, a clause on private property, and most significantly a new clause permitting the extension of the presidential period from six to seven years and the right of indefinite re-election for public officials, including the president.

The campaign was intense and very long, but for the first time since coming to power Chávez lost a vote, albeit narrowly. At first magnanimous in his response, he later described it as 'a shitty victory', an extremely uncharacteristic display of irritation. But rather than having been beaten by an opposition campaign, with its emphasis on a defence of private property which was wholly unnecessary since there was no threat to individual properties or indeed private ownership as a whole, he had lost a significant number of his own supporters. Abstention rates were high. In part, it could be argued, this was because of unease about an endlessly prolonged presidency, even Chávez's, but there was greater concern about the clause as it affected a number of very unpopular state governors and local mayors.

The reality was that the material conditions of the majority were beginning to deteriorate. The Missions were often unable to cope and rarely hit their targets; inflation was rising beyond the already high levels of previous years, and shortages of basic goods on supermarket shelves were becoming commonplace. The goods would then reappear later with higher price tags. It was the responsibility of the private supermarket chains, of course, but the government seemed unable to exercise any form of control over them. In the streets garbage was accumulating alarmingly and the incidence of violence was rising too. Chávez's supporters blamed the disruption on the right, who were certainly happy to exploit the discontent and unease it caused. But these problems were also the result of the financial mismanagement, bureaucratic inefficiency and corruption of government, local and national, and of the absence of any kind of strategic planning on its part. And the complex and not very well explained structural reforms did not appear to address any of these pressing issues.

The hope that workers would become more directly involved in the organisation of production in this new twenty-first-century socialism were also disappointed. The new union federation UNT, born in 2006 amid great hopes, was soon paralysed by internal disagreements and disabled by the refusal of the Labour Ministry to work with anyone other than the Bolivarian Federation of Labour (FBT), which was tightly controlled from above. And Chávez's intial enthusiasm for some kind of workers' self-management, exemplified by the Alcasa aluminium processing plant in Puerto Ordaz, was rapidly waning. According to Carlos Lanz, 'they treated us [in Alcasa] as an experiment', and then lost interest. Chávez's original enthusiasm for workers' control was expressed in October 2005 at a Latin American Meeting of Occupied and Recovered Factories. Yet he never returned to the issue.[7] Indeed in an *Aló Presidente* broadcast during a strike of workers on the Caracas metro he attacked the strikers and trade unionists in general for their selfish concern with their own wages. Yet his emphasis on participatory democracy remained a central theme of his public utterances. This was the Bolivarian paradox, as Iain Bruce calls it in the perceptive conclusion to his book. How is it possible for a movement from below to develop an independent collective leadership in a political culture completely dominated by a single individual? The communal councils clearly offered one opportunity, but the initiative proved unable to break through the blocks and obstacles placed in their way by the existing state and provincial structures and the interests they represented. And there was now a further block – the bureaucratic layer that had emerged *with* Chávez, and against the old order, who were now defending their own interests at the expense of the majority. If Chávez knew about their corruption (and everyone else seemed to, at least anecdotally) he did nothing to limit their powers. And when the occasional honest politician, like Minister of Consumer Affairs, Eduardo Samán, did emerge and began to act against the speculators and their allies he was quickly and summarily removed. The problem then is two-fold; good people with integrity are marginalised and there is no continuity in government with the single exception of Chávez himself. It was hard to avoid the conclusion I drew in 2008,[8] that Chávez had become a prisoner of what was called 'the endogenous right', whose power derived from the very practices of patronage and corruption that Chávez had vowed to eliminate when he was first elected, which he had patently failed to do, despite his promise early in 2008 to embark on a period of 'rectification and revision' (a phrase once again redolent of Fidel).

The regional and state elections for 2008 brought little comfort for Chávez. As the election approached it was presented once again as a vote of confidence in Chávez himself; the individual candidates were surrounded by images of the President and his attendance at their election rallies to the point of exhaustion was the only guarantee of their victory, especially given the arbitrary and undemocratic way in which candidates had been selected. In one sense, the PSUV had very little alternative; since the party members had not had any opportunity to discuss policy, and the leadership had not produced one, the only option was to emphasise the Chávez factor. And Chávez himself did not demur.

In the event, 57 per cent of the vote went to PSUV, but the picture was more complicated than it seemed. The right won five critical state governorships, including the emblematic state of Miranda where Diosdado Cabello, the most powerful member of the new bureaucracy, was unable to convince voters that they should support him. The states of Carabobo, oil and coal rich Zulia and the border state of Táchira went to the opposition and so, critically, did the mayoralty of Greater Caracas. The elections were marked by violence too – attacks on Cuban doctors, and the murder of three leading trade unionists involved in strikes. On the land, the endless battle between landowners and peasant farmers continued to leave a toll of death behind. And low-level civil servants were subject to threats and reprisals wherever the right returned to the town halls.

Rafael Uzcátegui's insightful book, *Venezuela: The Revolution as Spectacle*, is a carefully researched account of a deteriorating situation, growing worse when the oil price fell in 2009, veiled by an almost exclusive focus on Hugo Chávez. The revolution had become Chávez, and his words and discourse the reality which everyone, friends and enemies alike, engaged with. This was certainly helped by the growing network of communications media with a specifically Chavista orientation, and the equally intense denunciation in many of those media of any critical or questioning responses to his vision. Two daily television programmes exemplified the problem – the late night chat show hosted by Mario Silva and *La hojilla*. Both dealt in the currency of vulgarity and crude personal attacks that make any serious political debate impossible.[9] The official inflation rate for 2009 was around 26 per cent, but it was common knowledge that the actual inflation rate was far higher, particularly for food. The basket of basic goods cost more than the minimum wage, though disaster was averted by the presence of Mercal and other subsidised agencies. In fact Pdvsa had created its own food distribution agency, Pdval, presumably in response to Mercal's shortcomings. Yet it too was discredited when its Cuban directors were found to be dealing on the black market with their supplies. This was never properly explained, although it was common knowledge; more importantly the costs of what seemed to be a series of emergency responses rather than a strategic plan were never revealed.

Cases of internal corruption elsewhere in the state and among high-ranking personnel emerged throughout 2009; their resignations or replacement were announced but explanations were rarely given. They simply melted away.

Hugo Chávez, meanwhile, remained popular but seemed to be spending significantly more time on the international stage. The creation of new economic relationships with China, Russia and

Iran, but also with Colombia, Argentina and Brazil, brought home dramatically the dilemma of the political project that Chávez had set in motion in 1998. For while the creation of a bloc of nations may well have given them a little more weight in the global economy, the laws of motion of that economy still prevailed. And despite all the assurances to the contrary, these were alliances between national states whose political character was widely different; it was not a relationship between its peoples. Thus while on the world stage the alliances with Libya or Syria or Zimbabwe could well have served the purposes of exchange and mutual advantage in the world market, they inhibited any comment on, for example, the absence in those countries of the human rights to which Chávez himself was committed. The realpolitik of states flew in the face of the solidarity of exploited peoples.

In the end those relationships allowed economic growth and provided Venezuela with alternative sources for its imports and alternative markets for its oil (though the United States remained the major consumer of Venezuelan oil). But the economic *development* that had been promised from the beginning, the diversification of the economy and the creation of new industries that could supply domestic needs and help to reduce the astonishingly high level of imports, did not materialise. Most significantly, there was no increase in agricultural investment and production to address the fact that Venezuela still imported over 80 per cent of its food. By 2008, the Bolivarian revolution was facing an economic and a political crisis. Chávez's popularity was still undiminished, but his government was increasingly criticised. The Misiones were not functioning well; corruption and mismanagement were undermining their original purposes and Radio Bemba (as word of mouth is called) was accumulating anecdotal evidence of their failure (aside from the relentless attacks on the scheme by the right who always characterised the Missions as Cuban intervention).

The 'endogenous right' as the Chavista bureaucracy was called, was visibly gaining power. As ministers came and went apparently on a presidential whim, a core of leading people remained at their posts and wielded increasing power. Diosado Cabello, Rafael Ramírez, Jesse Chacón to name but a few were not only politically influential and occupying leading positions in the PSUV – their economic weight was growing exponentially too. They were not just functionaries, still less a collection of individuals. Each controlled economic and political structures in an increasingly intimate relationship with the military, who were occupying increasing numbers of leading positions. Together they were a new business and financial class who could and did work in conjunction with the powerful private capitalists of the country. Luis Tascón's criticisms of their role were withering. Their financial, political and organisational control of the institutions of the state – and the PSUV was an institution of the state, with no semblance of independence – made the kind of grassroots, participatory democracy that Chávez symbolised a mere abstraction. There were no mechanisms for their rule or their decisions to be challenged either within or outside the state. As Tascón pointed out, of the 5.7 million members of PSUV only 2 million voted in the 2008 elections. What then did membership mean to the others?

Acción Democrática (like the Mexican PRI) recruited its supporters on the basis of a promise of advantage, financial or political. The PSUV was increasingly doing the same, and renovating and recreating the networks of favouritism and clientilism which were the source of popular rage against the old state. Its predecessor, the MVR, had been riven with contradictions and opportunism – yet it had successfully mobilised large numbers behind the Bolivarian project. PSUV had not arisen out of mass mobilisations, nor grown from the ground up. On the contrary – its leaders existed before its members and many of those who joined did so for their own interests rather than out of conviction. Yet the party also attracted the most committed activists, though their numbers were very small compared to earlier years, the campaign around 2004 recall referendum for example, which had involved very large numbers. And Tascón was only the first to be expelled for his critical comments, soon after the PSUV was created – but he was by no means the last to be subject to this bureaucratic, as opposed to political, method.

Tascón commented that Chávez was most successful where there was social conflict; that after 2006 there was social peace and the rhetoric of confrontation ceased to function well. That was reflected in the clumsy and depoliticised campaign on the constitutional amendments which Chávez may or may not have chosen, but which focused on him as an individual and spent a great deal of time discussing love and unity. It was Chávez's good fortune that the right had neither social programme nor political strategy but only a yearning to return to power and its advantages. Yet the campaign did express something important; on Chávez's own part, a kind of complacency combined with anger at what must have seemed to him, at some points, like a betrayal of him by the people. That was the import of his remark about 'a shitty victory'. Beyond that there was the thesis advanced by many critical voices within the ruling party and the Bolivarian circles; that Chávez had been, as it were, kidnapped by the new Chavista right, imprisoned by them because of their economic and political power, together with the capacity to flatter and cajole the emotional and ultimately rather self-important Chávez.

The future of the revolution would now depend on the ability of its leaders and activists to define a political strategy that corresponded to the central presence of the mass movement, and that built on the experience of democracy in the struggles that had brought Chávez to power and kept him there. As Iain Bruce put it

> The institutional levers of power in Venezuela – including the office of the presidency itself – remain institutionally located, even 'trapped', within the old administrative structures. This has been part of Chávez's own paradox. He promotes, sometimes more sometimes less, these revolutionary initiatives – the possible seeds of an alternative state – from his office in Miraflores, the emblematic edifice of the old one.[10]

For its part, the opposition concentrated its fire on Chávez too, freezing the political process as an endless recycling of arguments for and against Chávez himself. The right-wing media were extraordinary in this period – chat shows, interviews and political commentaries centred obsessively on the leader, conducting earnest discussions with psychiatrists about his mental state and exchanging anecdotes about his private life. There was curiously little of either when it came to the new bureaucracy, the powerful people at the top.

Did that suggest an implicit fusion of economic interests between private capital and the bureaucracy? Or more profoundly, was this an oblique sign of where the economy was also going – towards a strong state as an economic actor working in concert with private capital to create a state-led economy? There were certainly indications that something like that was happening – the joint enterprises set up between Pdvsa and oil multinationals like ChevronTexaco to develop the Orinoco Basin's enormous reserves were a powerful sign of things to come. The new economic agreements with China, Iran and Russia, among others, served the Venezuelan state capitalist economy – but they could not be explained or justified in any sense at all as contributions to the *revolution*. They were, indeed, commercial and financial arrangements that diversified Venezuela's external dependency, but did not eliminate it. The Orinoco agreements were not just significant because they linked Russian and Chinese state capital with Venezuela, but because they also indicated a direction of travel – collaboration with capital, in its many forms, based on the continuing role of Venezuela as an oil producer, essentially as a monoproducer. What was being brought into Venezuela were plants producing basically consumer items, above all cars, telephones and computers, which would not transform industrial production in the country.

These facilities were not transferred to Venezuela as acts of international solidarity; their purpose was to extract maximum profits from the workers who produced the goods. And it was to be expected that, as in any other capitalist system, the workers would resist exploitation through their own organisations – the trade unions. In a society recently declared to be socialist, they would have had a right to expect support and a defence of their collective rights. But for the workers at the Mitsubishi plant in Valencia, for example, the consequence of their collective defence was the death of nine trade unionists at the hands of armed thugs with the collusion of local (Chavista) authorities. And the independent trade union federation, the UNT, had been systematically sabotaged by Chávez's personal appointees at the Ministry, culminating in an incident in which leaders of the union of civil servants were locked in to the Ministry while its incumbent refused to meet with them.

It was perhaps not surprising that a man whose experience of organisation was within a hierarchical command structure, who had no trade union experience, and who had come from a system in which the trade union leaders were collaborators with the corrupt bureaucracy, should have been suspicious. But only a year or two before that, he had supported Carlos Lanz's initiative to introduce workers' self-management, for all its contradictions, into key areas of the economy. While some foreign commentators suggested that Chávez had initiated large scale expropriations, in fact nationalisations were very few, specific to enterprises that had been abandoned or had stopped functioning, and they were compensated at market rates. And the occupied factories, like Venapal and Sanitarios Maracay, which had become iconic at an earlier stage, were effectively abandoned and state support withdrawn. Increasingly, what initiatives there were, were taken independently by particular groups of workers, like those in the salt and the fish-packing plants.

More generally, the question of political organisation as an expression of the rather imprecise notion of *poder popular* was never addressed, either by Chávez or within the PSUV. In part that can be explained by the particular experience of Chávez and those around him, and the discredit in which the old bourgeois political parties were held. The parties of the left, for their part, had endlessly fragmented and those that mantained some degree of coherence, like the Venezuelan Communist Party, had had the ground taken from under them, by the creation of the PSUV. Iain Bruce (writing in 2007) offers one explanation: 'The central problem for the Bolivarian movement ... is ... how do you get round the existing apparatus when you first came to power *through* it ... especially when it has become increasingly clear that a number of those inhabiting the old edifice alongside Chávez, who helped him move in ... have absolutely no wish to move out.'[11]

In its beginning the *proceso* gave an answer; this was a process of shifting power from the state to the people. As Bruce wrote, the test of whether this was true or not would be whether the communal councils were genuine organs of direct democracy, the strengthening and deepening of workers' organisations, and the creation of a political organisation at the heart of the system that could politically and organisationally prepare a new kind of state and the destruction of the old.

The concentration of power in the hands of a 'new political class' was the alternative to the participatory democracy promised by Chávez and the 1999 Constitution. Its consequence was an increasing demobilisation and demoralisation of the grassroots. When Chávez announced the formation of the *consejos comunales* early in 2006, a surge of optimism followed; perhaps this signalled a return to the promised participation and grassroots democracy. But while they were established and in many cases functioned well as conduits carrying information to local government, they were in no sense organs of popular power. Many indeed were not supportive of the government. In the general context of centralised control and power administered consistently and relentlessly from above, they remained another unfulfilled promise. And their funding proved to be another means for the endogenous right to consolidate their power, distributing resources to win allegiance. Inside the PSUV there were serious arguments; a number of candidates imposed by the bureaucracy were rejected by the grassroots, but their protests were largely ignored and the official candidates imposed. They in their turn were the guarantee of the bureaucracy's continuing control.

By 2009 the economic realities, the consequences of a world recession which the Venezuelan government had confidently said would not be coming home, began to resonate in Venezuela. The slight fall in the price of oil created enormous tensions and Venezuela rushed to convince OPEC to reduce production. Inflation levels, already high, were hitting new peaks; while the official figure hovered around 30 per cent, the real figure was much higher in areas like food and transport, where arbitrary price rises imposed by the bus owners or in the wake of sudden and unexplained shortages in supermarkets were making day to day survival harder for the poor and the working class. In the countryside, the battle over land was claiming more and more victims as peasant organisations fought, and many died, in struggles with the landed oligarchy.

The violence and insecurity in the country was escalating, even if the right-wing media did trade on them to intensify the atmosphere of anxiety and apprehension in the country. The infrastructure was visibly falling apart, as the rubbish piling up in the streets testified.

Where was Chávez in all this? His *Aló Presidente* shows were broadcast with absolute regularity. He visited farms and cooperatives, hugged babies and announced encouraging figures for the economy. Yet oil now represented 96 per cent of export earnings, the highest level yet and the model socialist enterprises and cooperatives, like the Fabricio Ojeda project, which were offered as examples of a new social economy were failing everywhere.

Figure 7.1 Chávez at an advanced stage of his illness (© Luis Noguera)

In 2010 there was a prolonged electricity crisis, clearly the result of long-term inefficiencies and the endemic corruption.[12] It was becoming increasingly urgent for Venezuela to integrate its activities with its new economic partners like China and Russia. For the left,

Chávez's change of heart on his support for the Colombian Farc, the guerrilla organisation that had begun as a network of peasant self-defence organisations in 1948,[13] posed a serious problem. When the new president of Colombia, Santos, who had been the Defence Minister under the previous government of Uribe, the US's firmest ally in Latin America and a byword for state terror, took office, Chávez made clear overtures towards him – and distanced himself from the Farc. He gave as his reasons that the guerrilla strategy was no longer relevant, but there were other considerations underpinning his active support of the peace process and his increasing intimacy with Santos. The reasons were economic, the gas pipeline through the Caribbean which would be jointly owned, and economic cooperation between the two nations. Chávez's failure to condemn the coup in Honduras in 2010 was further evidence of a shifting position.

The discontents were becoming increasingly clear – in the falling audiences for *Aló Presidente*, in the increasingly loud complaints about the bureaucracy, in the unacceptable levels of inflation and the failure to deal with the violence which was now spreading hand in hand with drug trafficking and reaching frightening proportions. Venezuelans were used to Chávez's absence as he travelled abroad. But it was clear by 2011 that he was ill, and spending large amounts of time in Cuba for treatment. What was more significant was that government virtually ceased to function in his absence. He was less and less in control of state or government, yet those who were steering Venezuela towards a new state capitalism which would reintegrate the country with the world market under slightly altered terms were inhibited about acting in his absence. Chávez was their validation and their shield against popular demands and collective criticism. His speeches and his tireless communication with the public, to which Twitter was now added, maintained an illusion of collaboration – but it had no organisational form and no corresponding political strategy. Behind the rhetoric of Bolivarian revolution lay chaos, corruption, and a systematic depoliticisation of the population.

When Chávez came to power, and as he faced the repeated assaults of the right, there was debate, popular mobilisation, an impulse to change and seek a new future, the world that was there to win. It was a message that evoked enthusiasm and hope in millions, and that was vindicated by the movements that erupted across Latin America and took up the demand for a twenty-first-century socialism. And yet, as the election of 2012 approached, and Chávez spoke of 'a revolution within the revolution', it was largely an empty gesture, when the movement he had created in the name of participatory democracy had produced a system as rigidly controlled and as corrupt as the one he had replaced. And as the gap between the promised social advances and the economic realities of survival in a globalised world grew wider, the new left governments of Latin America reluctantly or not bent to the neo-liberalism that shaped the world market. Much had changed, yet Venezuela, Bolivia and Ecuador remained producers of primary materials for the dominant centres of the world system, now including China and Russia.

It is a truism to say that power corrupts, that the acclaim of millions and the conviction that you can change the world on their behalf and in their stead, will bring unbearable pressures on political leaders who are not, in their beginnings, autocrats or authoritarians. The confusions that Chávez's contradictory speeches produced in his listeners were an expression of his own unresolved conflicts. At some point, perhaps after 2006, Chávez should have given way to the movement he set out to generate. Chavismo without Chávez would have given a very different sense to the chants of the huge crowds who attended the election rallies after he was re-elected in 2012 but was too ill to attend, who shouted 'We are all Chávez'. They were right, but they had surrendered the right to make the revolution to an individual who could not resolve the paradox of an individual acting for the collective good. Demoralised and demobilised, the only functioning collective when Hugo Chávez died was the bureaucracy who had used his name to usurp power.

In the latter part of 2012, Chávez was largely absent from Venezuela while he submitted to increasingly aggressive cancer treatment in Cuba. News about his condition was very scarce and sparked endless speculation and rumour. In the meantime, government ground to a virtual halt. There were two pending elections. The presidential election on 8 October gave Chávez over eight million votes, 55 per cent of the total. His opponent Henrique Capriles was a representative of the most powerful sections of the bourgeoisie, but he was younger than the characteristically older AD candidates of earlier times. He was white and good-looking, as indeed were most opposition candidates in the later regional elections in December. His performance was creditable and although the margin was undeniable, Chávez's result was less encouraging than it seemed. The campaign, meanwhile, had been entirely conducted around Chávez, for and against. He returned to Cuba immediately after the election, and returned only briefly thereafter.

The December regional elections, for governors and mayors, were more revealing. It was noticeable, for example, how many gubernatorial candidates of the PSUV were ex-ministers; those who were not had been hand picked, reputedly by Chávez but in fact by the bureaucracy, often in the teeth of local opposition. A particular case in point was the candidate for Merida, a young geographer who was rejected by the local party, yet imposed. But this election too was conducted entirely around the figure of Chávez, despite his absence.

The results of those elections were encouraging for the PSUV. The right lost all but one of the governorships it had won four years earlier, with only Capriles winning Miranda – mark of the continuing unpopularity of Cabello. More significantly, nine of the 22 Chavista governors were serving or retired military men. As January 2013 approached, it was clear that Chávez himself would not be present to take his oath of office. There were frenzied discussions about the legal and constitutional position, and whether he could be elected to the presidency if he was not physically present. In the end, these internecine squabbles were resolved by the mass of the people.

It was deeply moving to see the hundreds of thousands who filled the street to take the oath on Chávez's behalf. Two months later, on 5 March, they would leave their homes to join the public mourning after the announcement of Chávez's death from cancer. Their tears were genuine grief. Whatever the doubts, criticisms or ambiguities, Hugo Chávez had changed his country, and possibly Latin America, for ever.

7

The Legacy of Hugo Chávez

The Boulders in the Road

Before his death, Hugo Chávez had nominated Nicolás Maduro, his vice-president and for some years before that his foreign minister, as his successor. In a democracy a dynastic handover of this kind is extremely problematic, but in the emotional turmoil that followed Chávez's death, that issue was forgotten. In the event, of course, Maduro thus became the official candidate of the PSUV. The PSUV's structures, however, did not allow of any real process of nomination and selection of a new candidate, even had Chávez not given Maduro his personal seal of approval. In the six years since its foundation it had become very clear that the party was an apparatus of power, the political organisation of the new bureaucracy that had emerged in that same period. That is not to say that Maduro would not have won the approval of a majority of party members; but we cannot be certain of that, since his candidacy was never tested. He did receive the enthusiastic support of significant numbers of activists, nonetheless, as a posthumous gesture to Hugo Chávez, rather than as an expression of Maduro's personal support.

Inevitably, the election campaign that followed the period of mourning, in April 2013, was dominated by the deceased leader on both sides of the contest. Henrique Capriles Radonski had emerged as the preferred candidate of the right; his appearance reflected the modern, the cosmopolitan, and represented the largely white bourgeoisie and the middle class who liked to think of themselves that way. It was a pointed contrast to the charismatic Chávez, whom the right had always characterised by his racial characteristics and his popular way of speaking. In an election dominated more than ever by the mass media, appearance would be everything. And the truth

Figure 8.1   Public grief at Chávez's death (© Luis Noguera)

was that Maduro could not match the charisma, the communicative skill or the overt charm of his predecessor. He was quieter, more considered, and his speaking style and language were more formal, despite his working-class background.

For the moment, however, he could claim to continue the tradition of Chávez, just as Capriles continued the concentration of twelve previous years of propaganda against Chávez, his leadership and his Cuban connections. The result was that the election campaign maintained the Manichaean, confrontational method of the many elections in which Chávez had participated, and in which he denounced the right and their connections to Washington with colourful epithets and withering sarcasm. But it was not Maduro's style, and it was largely left to the rotweilers of Chavismo, like the television columnist Mario Silva, to conduct the more brutal campaigning.

Maduro had the advantage, however, of Chávez's last political document, his *Socialist Plan of the Nation 2013–2019*. It was a fairly lengthy document, focusing on five areas – national sovereignty and independence, the socialist character of the revolution, Latin American integration, the necessity of a multi-polar world, and the environment.[1] In its content and the key issues it identifies, it is a continuation of the previous six-year plan. It also repeats many of the previous plan's aspirations and undertakings, without addressing the reasons why the objectives of the earlier document remained unfulfilled – why the housing plan never approached its target, why the Barrio Adentro building programme fell so short of its target and why at the same time the public sector hospitals had fallen into such catastrophic disrepair.

Politically, it remains centrally committed to the original vision of a participatory democracy, expressed mainly in the communal councils and the rather ill-defined co-management arrangements to which the plan alludes. Yet these same aspirations had manifestly failed in the previous regime. The communal councils were functioning in many cases as forms of municipal government, indenting for government funding for specific projects or implementing government plans. But this was a very long way from *poder popular*, the direct decision-making power of the people to determine their own future. A benevolent government taking into account public opinion while taking its own decisions independently of the grassroots is, at best, reformism. It could be argued, of course, that there exists a mass political party where those arguments can take place. The reality of the PSUV, however, was that the party is a top-down structure whose activists execute decisions but do not make them. When the local organisation in Mérida, for example, protested at the imposition of a gubernatorial candidate with no base or experience in the area, they were overruled.

Education, morality, ethical standards, which the Plan demands, are all necessary but not sufficient conditions for a participatory democracy; without access to power they do not go beyond personal values. In any event, what defines a socialist society is the transformation of capitalist social and productive relations. The Plan envisages a future in which Venezuela continues to be dependent on oil production to produce the revenues with which to import all the country's other requirements – from its new trading partners, China, Russia and Iran. That might lessen the dependency on the United States, but it will not change the relationship between Venezuela and its partners in a global market where the capitalist law of value prevails. The promise inherent in Chávez's various initiatives towards Latin American integration – ALBA, Unasur (the alternative to the South American trade area, Mercosur, which Venezuela also joined), Celac, Petrocaribe (the organisation of Caribbean oil consumers) and the rest – was that they would foster a different relationship, of exchange and interaction rather than exploitation. Yet it is the case that not just Venezuela, but the other progressive regimes of Latin America, like Bolivia and Ecuador, are themselves trapped in admittedly new dependencies which oblige them to continue to provide raw materials in exchange for manufactured goods, technology and the like. And in Venezuela's case, for food too, more than 80 per cent of which is still imported. The increased demand for food, of course, reflects the better standard of living currently enjoyed by all Venezuelans – but it also exposes the fact that little or nothing has been done so far to raise agricultural productivity or to invest in large scale development in the sector. The Second Plan undertakes to do that, but unless the reasons why it failed to happen the first time around are addressed, it seems unlikely that the crisis of agriculture will be resolved.

The plans for new economic structures, including cooperatives, workers self-management, nationalisations, and socialist enterprises, understandably created much excitement among observers of the Bolivarian process outside Venezuela as well as among Venezuelan supporters of Chávez. But the undoubtedly good intentions behind them came to very little in the end. The explanation for that is complex, but in part it has to do with the lack of a strategic view; decisions tended to be made for short term, expedient reasons, only to be pushed aside by other more urgent considerations. The truth is that the Plan deals in generalities, in no doubt honest statements of intent and aspirations. But even Chávez recognised, near the end of his life, that Venezuela remains a capitalist society; given the state's control of oil, the central motor of the economy, it is a state capitalism, but capitalist nonetheless. Pdvsa's management may now wear red baseball caps and use the discourse of socialism, but the experiment in workers' control of the corporation was abandoned when Rafael Ramírez came to be its president, in part because of its key role in the economy, and in part for political reasons – another manifestation of the paradox of Bolivarianism. The managers of the various state enterprises are now members of a new state bureaucracy, but it is one that is reproducing all the characteristics of the previous regimes – corruption, mismanagement, inefficiency and opacity – the complete opposite of the promised transparency that must accompany public accountability. The bureaucracy is effectively a new class which while not owning the means of production administers them in its own interests and for its own profit. And it is now the fundamental block to any socialist transformation.

Maduro's Challenge

In April 2013, Nicolas Maduro won the first presidential election since Chávez's death – but by a margin of only 1.8 per cent, the smallest in any election since 1998. In part this was because Maduro could not reproduce Chávez's relationship with his social base, nor enjoy his extraordinary credibility. But equally it was a reaction to the devaluation that preceded the elections by a few weeks, and to the apparent inability of government to control the price inflation that seemed increasingly out of control. Even when the problems and failures of Chavismo, and the excessive power of the *boliburguesía* or the new bureaucracy was the talk of every market place, Chávez was exempted from responsibility for its emergence. Maduro will not be given the same concessions. He has to win a support which Chávez, mistakenly and with sometimes very negative consequences, took for granted.

Immediately after the election, the Capriles camp launched a vicious and violent campaign, including hunger strikes and arson, as well as the murder of eight Chavista activists, claiming fraud. They were enthusiastically supported in their allegations by Washington, but every other international agency and observer praised the honesty of the electoral process.

Part of Chávez's legacy has been a series of unanswered questions. How will Venezuelan state capitalism, with its still immensely powerful private capitalists untouched by twelve years of a Bolivarian revolution, transform itself into a socialist economy? Maduro's negotiations with Mendoza and Zuloaga, two of the 'four horsemen of the apocalypse' (the name popularly given to the four wealthiest private capitalists in Venezuela) suggest a very different direction, since his solution to the food crisis in whose creation they are clearly complicit is to offer to invest state funds in their enterprises in exchange for increases and improvements in supply. That will not only make them richer, it will also consolidate the current system, and this in a situation in which the devaluation announced at the very beginning of his administration cut the value of wages at a stroke and with it the standard of living of the majority. The beneficiaries, ironically enough, will be those very people who have raised prices even further by creating artificial shortages who will now receive state subsidies.

How will people's power, the participatory democracy the promise of which won Chávez the allegiance of millions, be realised in the next period? The Second Plan offers a continuation – but of what? The United Socialist Party of Venezuela, to quote Guillermo Almeyra[2] is not socialist, nor is it united. A twenty-first century socialism, whatever its specific characteristics, requires an organisation that can mobilise and coordinate the Chavistas at the grassroots, the potential subjects of any socialist revolution. PSUV belongs to the bureaucracy. A new socialist organisation, whatever its form or its single or multiple ideologies, cannot by definition be formed by that layer. It must be independent, critical, and visionary. No existing current can claim the right to ownership of that project because it has to emerge out of the experience and consciousness of the movements of the poor and the working class. Its form and content will be determined in the struggles to come.

What then is the legacy of Hugo Chávez? Like the man himself, it is contradictory. His role in the final defeat of the *puntofijista* system and his commitment to a new radical liberal constitution embracing human and collective rights and the right to an authentic national independence inspired a generation. It gave a shape and a direction to the hopes and demands of a majority of his fellow countrymen and women who for four decades had been marginalised and ignored. He recuperated a national historical memory, and gave new value to a popular culture that had been overwhelmed by a Western consumer culture that carried within it the values of an aggressive capitalism.

The musicians and writers of Venezuela found a champion in him, and the marginalised indigenous peoples have had their history celebrated for the first time.[3] He articulated a denunciation of neo-liberalism that every people that had been subject to its cruelties and depredations could recognise and echo.

Sometimes individuals can take on key roles in those historical moments when there are no organised collective expressions of alternative possibilities. Chávez emerged into the limelight at just such a moment, and led a fierce battle against an implacable class enemy. The votes he received were indications of how much that role was valued in its time. But at a critical moment participatory democracy could only have a meaning if power was passed from his hands into the possession of a collective protagonist and its political expressions encouraged and supported. At that moment Chávez pulled the reins of power back towards himself, and the opportunity was lost. What was created instead was a mirage, an appearance of participation that veiled a concentration of power in Chávez himself and in the bureaucracy that was growing in his shadow. It is unclear whether he failed to see it until it was too late, or whether he was complicit in the formation of a new ruling layer which eventually reproduced the corruption, inefficiency and clientilism that had so enraged the people of Venezuela. Perhaps Chávez was just human enough to be flattered into believing in his own indispensability. And that was perhaps the other side of the humane qualities that had won him the affection of those who wept when he died.

For those who want to pick up again the baton of twenty-first-century socialism, the task now is to rebuild the mass movement and its political expressions, to refuse the stratagems and ruses of a new ruling group and to prepare for the next opportunity that history offers to sweep away global capitalism, armed with the lessons, the warnings and the inspirations that are Hugo Chávez's legacy.

Notes

Introduction

1. It was Bolívar who described himself as 'a man for the difficult times'. Chávez rediscovered those words, which seemed peculiarly appropriate to his own experience.
2. Rory Carroll, *Comandante: The life and Legacy of Hugo Chávez*, Edinburgh, 2013.

Chapter 1

1. Bart Jones, *Hugo! The Hugo Chávez Story from Mud Hut to Perpetual Revolution*, London, 2008.
2. *Caudillo* is a term used widely in Latin America. It refers to local military leaders with political as well as military power.
3. As Douglas Bravo pointed out to me, in Colombia you could not even aspire to the officer class unless you had several surnames and a letter of recommendation from the Archbishop!
4. C. Marcano and A. Barrera Tyszka, *Hugo Chávez sin uniforme*, Caracas, 2004, p.63. (Translated as *Hugo Chávez: The definitive Biography of Venezuela's Controversial President*, New York, 2007.)
5. The failure of Sinamos left a generation of young professionals angry and disillusioned: they would later form the base of the Shining Path organisation.
6. Marcano and Tyszka, *Hugo Chávez sin uniforme*, p. 72.
7. This issue is the theme of a series of essays on the relationship between social movements and the military from the Commune to Egypt in H. Barekat and M. Gonzalez (eds), *Arms and the People*, London, 2012.
8. This account of these events owes much to Douglas Bravo, the revolutionary leader who participated in the January actions as a workers leader and a communist, and to whom I will return later. See Douglas Bravo and Argelia Melet, 'A la nación venezolana', in *La otra crisis*, Caracas, 1991, pp. 125–44.
9. Personal interview, Caracas, 2011.

10. See Pedro Pablo Linarez: *La lucha armada en Venezuela*, Caracas Bolívariana, 2006.
11. It is what is known as 'the Dutch disease'.

Chapter 2

1. As reported by C. Marcano and A. Barrera Tyszka, in *Hugo Chávez sin uniforme*, Caracas, 2004, p. 77.
2. Gabriel García Márquez, 'El enigma de los dos Chávez', in *Cambio* (Bogotá), Feb 1999, www.redvoltaire.net/article84.html. This article is often cited, especially by opponents of Chávez wishing to represent him as schizophrenic in his attitudes.
3. The Armed Forces of National Liberation (FALN) included members of a range of organisations in the early- to mid-sixties. But the left organisations split over the question of the armed struggle through the latter years of the decade. Teodoro Petkoff and Pompeyo Marquez, for example, at the time members of the Communist Party, published a document highly critical of the guerrilla strategy in 1965. The debate arose in the MIR too, and the majority of the guerrilla fronts had effectively ceased to operate by 1969.
4. Margarita López Maya, quoted in Richard Gott, *In the Shadow of the Liberator*, London, 2000, p. 136. Gott goes on to give a brief account of the rise of Causa R (pp. 136–42).
5. See Nikolas Kozloff, *Hugo Chávez: Oil Politics and the Challenge to the U.S.*, New York, 2006, pp. 42–4.
6. The 200 referred to the years since Bolívar's birth.
7. Gott, *Shadow of the Liberator*, p. 40.
8. See John Lynch, *Simón Bolívar: A Life*, New Haven/London, 2006. p. 73.
9. Lynch, *Simón Bolívar*, p. 77.
10. Lynch, *Simón Bolívar*, pp. 201–2.
11. The last part of his life is narrated with poignancy in Gabriel García Márquez's *The General in his Labyrinth*.
12. See Gott, *Shadow of the Liberator*, p. 107.
13. Gott, *Shadow of the Liberator*, pp. 108–17.
14. Jose R. Revenga, *La hacienda pública de Venezuela de 1828 a 1839*, Pedro Grases and M. perez Vila Caracas (eds), 1953, pp. 95–6. Quoted in Lynch, *Simón Bolívar*, pp. 164–5. The letter containing this advice was dated 5 May 1829.

15. In an odd aside in his conversations with Marta Haernecker, Chávez first of all claims that his movement did not use the word 'revolutionary' until much later. The available literature suggests this is not true. M. Haernecker, *Understanding the Venezuelan Revolution*, New York, 2005, p. 31.

16. See Bart Jones' slightly colourful account in *Hugo! The Hugo Chávez Story from Mud Hut to Perpetual Revolution*, London, 2008.

17. Haernecker, *Understanding the Venezuelan Revolution*, p. 30.

18. See Douglas Bravo and Argelia Melet, *La otra crisis*, Caracas, 1991, and my interview with Bravo in H. Barekat and M. Gonzalez (eds), *Arms and the People*, London, 2012.

Chapter 3

1. Rafael Uzcátegui, *Venezuela: la revolución como espectáculo: una crítica anarquista al gobierno Bolivariano*, Caracas, 2010, p. 182.

2. Michael McCaughan, *The Battle of Venezuela*, Seven Stories Press, 2005, p. 33.

3. As symbolised so powerfully in the 'plague of forgetfulness' that follows the massacre of striking banana workers in Gabriel García Márquez's masterpiece *One Hundred Years of Solitude*.

4. Roland Denis, *Las tres repúblicas*, Caracas, 2011. p. 49.

5. Richard Gott, *In the Shadow of the Liberator*, London, 2000, p. 46.

6. M. Haernecker, *Understanding the Venezuelan Revolution*, New York, 2005, p. 32.

7. Gott, *In the Shadow of the Liberator*, p. 48.

8. Douglas Bravo, 'The civic-military alliance in Venezuela 1958–1990', in H. Barekat and M. Gonzalez (eds), *Arms and the people*, London, 2013, p. 285.

9. As set out in his book *La IV Republica*.

10. C. Marcano and A. Barrera Tyszka, in *Hugo Chávez sin uniforme*, Caracas, 2004 p. 105.

11. In conversation with Blanco Muñoz. Quoted in Marcano and Barrera Tyszka, *Hugo Chávez*, p. 107.

12. There will be more to say later about the role of Cuba, but Pérez had traded with Cuba on very favourable conditions for them, exporting cement for example.

13. Chávez's version is that they had prepared arms for civilian groups but they had failed to appear. Bravo denies that.

14. Roland Denis, *Los fabricantes de la rebelión*, Caracas, 2001, p. 31.

15. It is now a museum commemorating and preserving that experience.

16. See Marcano and Barrera Tyszka, *Hugo Chávez*, p. 146.

17. Telesur began broadcasting in October 2005, after several months of limited pilot programmes. It maintains a high journalistic standard in its news bulletins, and was perceived at the outset as a broadcaster serving Latin America as a whole – since Latin American events rarely registered in US or European media. The founding of Telesur did provoke hostile reactions in the US Senate, where accusations that its founding compromised freedom of expression in Venezuela were scarcely credible, given that the state controlled two TV channels, plus Telesur, while the 48 privately owned, freely available channels were universally hostile to Chávez.

18. Edgardo Lander 'Venezuelan social conflict in a global context', in *Latin American Perspectives*, vol. 32:2, issue 141, March 2005, pp. 24–6.

19. *Ibid.*, p. 27.

20. Luis Giusti would subsequently join the National Security Agency in Washington.

21. Haernecker, *Understanding the Venezuelan Revolution*, p.42, but with my retranslation – his words are mistranslated in the English language edition.

22. Bernal did not change his position and was marginalised within the MBR for some time as a result.

23. See C. Valencia Ramirez, 'Who are the Chavistas', in *Latin American Perspectives*, issue 142, vol. 32 no. 3 May, 2005, pp. 79–97.

24. See Marcano and Barrera Tyszka, *Hugo Chávez*, pp. 180–3.

Chapter 4

1. Luciano Wexell Severo, 'In Venezuela oil sows emancipation', www.venezuelanalysis.com/print.php?artno=1694.

2. M. Haernecker, *Understanding the Venezuelan Revolution*, New York, 2005, p.45. Yet it had not arisen in February 1992 and remained a very minor theme until this point.

3. Quoted in Néstor Francia, *¿Qué piensa Chávez?*, Caracas, 2003, pp. 60–1.

4. By 2004 that would have risen to 135 countries over 248 days.

5. Bernard Mommer, 'Subversive Oil', in Steve Ellner and Daniel Hellinger (eds), *Venezuelan Politics in the Chávez Era*, Boulder, 2003, p. 135.

6. Venezuelan oil still represented 15 per cent of total US consumption.

7. NACLA Report on the Americas, vol XXXIII no. 6, May/June 2000, p. 30.

8. Haernecker, *Understanding the Venezuelan Revolution*, p. 161.

9. The shock and horror expressed by a hostile foreign press was a little questionable given, for example, the enormous resources that the US president has to finance war without recourse to Congress.

10. Quote in Francia, *¿Qué piensa Chávez?*, pp. 17, 19.

11. C. Marcano and A. Barrera Tyszka, in *Hugo Chávez sin uniforme*, Caracas, 2004, p. 267.

12. *Ibid.*, p. 289.

13. This information and much that follows comes from the account by Germán Sánchez Otero, then the Cuban ambassador in Caracas, in *Abril sin censura*, Caracas, 2012.

14. On the experience of Popular Unity and the coup in Chile see P. O'Brien, J. Roddick and I. Roxborough, *State and Revolution in Chile*, London, 1975, and V. Figueroa Clark: *Salvador Allende*, London, 2013. The films of Patricio Guzmán tell the story of those events with insight and great emotional power – 'The battle of Chile' and 'Allende'.

15. The actual course of events, so maliciously distorted at the time, is painstakingly reconstructed in Angel Palacios' film *El puente de Llaguno*.

16. US ambassador David Shapiro was also a lunch guest.

17. Rod Stoneman, *Chávez: The Revolution will not be Televised: A Case Study of Politics and the Media*, London, 2008, contains a DVD of the original documentary by Kim Bartley and Donnacha O'Briain – it can also be seen on YouTube.

Chapter 5

1. M. McCaughan, *The Battle of Venezuela*, Seven Stories Press, London, 2005, p. 94.

2. Roland Denis, *Rebelión en proceso*, Caracas, n.d., p. 8.

3. The case of Bandera Roja is a complex one, and perplexing for external observers. Formed in 1970 as a guerrilla organisation, its positions were ultra left and sympathetic to Maoism. It continued from time to time its armed actions, while working at the same time principally among school and university students. It has been an implacable opponent of Chávez, to the degree that it has consistently worked with the right against him. Its discourse remains on the left, but its actions place it squarely with the right, and the extreme right at that. Their hostility to Chávez was justified by their description of him as a false communist. There was of course

an extensive and impassioned debate across the left about Chávez's policies and politics; but very few on the left allied with a right whose interests lay in the restoration of the political system which the majority of Venezuelans had rejected in voting for Chávez.

4. The battle against time and sabotage to 'restore the brains of Pdvsa' is told in a fascinating documentary *El rescate del cerebro de Pdvsa*, directed by Mark Villa and Primeras Voces and produced by Marianella Yanes and Lourdes Contreras in 2003.

5. Edgar Lander, 'Comentarios informales sobre la situación política venezolana', 3 January 2003.

6. In *El golpe fascista contra Venezuela*, Caracas, 2003, a compilation of Chávez's speeches during the bosses strike of 2002–03, p. 105.

7. According to a press release from the Venezuela Information Office.

8. Rafael Uzcátegui, *Venezuela, la revolución como espectáculo*, Caracas, 2010, pp. 140–3.

9. Chávez, quoted in Uzcátegui, *Venezuela*, p. 144.

10. Quoted in Uzcátegui, *Venezuela*, p. 150. Uzcátegui writes from an anarchist perspective, but his analysis of the Missions, their successes and failures, is carefully argued and well researched. See pp. 143–58.

11. His report was published as 'Venezuela's Path' on ZNet, 6 November 2005.

12. See Iain Bruce, *The Real Venezuela*, London, 2008. p. 110.

13. The participation of private capital in the economy was 64.7 per cent in 1998, and 70.9 per cent in 2008. Further, two days before the 2004 referendum Chávez had shown the press a US analysis which showed trade with Venezuela was now more stable than ten years earlier.

14. R. Gott, *Hugo Chávez and the Bolivarian Revolution*, London, 2005, p. 262.

15. Bart Jones, *Hugo! The Hugo Chávez Story from Mud Hut to Perpetual Revolution*, London, 2008.

Chapter 6

1. See Samuel Farber, *Cuba since the Revolution of 1959: A Critical Assessment*, Chicago, 2011.

2. R. Hernandez, *Las revelaciones de Luis Tascón*, Caracas, 2008, p. 37.

3. *Ibid.*, p. 60.

4. Tascón was to have the dubious distinction of being the first person expelled from the PSUV.

5. Gregory Wilpert, *Changing Venezuela by Taking Power*, London, 2007, p. 193.

6. García Guadilla, quoted in Rafael Uzcátegui, *Venezuela, la revolución como espectáculo*, Caracas, 2010, p. 206.

7. Iain Bruce, *The Real Venezuela*, London, 2008, p. 123.

8. M. Gonzalez, 'Ten years on: Venezuela at the crossroads', in *International Socialism Journal*, no. 121, Winter 2008, see www.isj.org.uk.

9. In fact both have been discredited more recently. Silva failed in his attempt to win a governorship and was then recorded speaking contemptuously of the government after which he was removed from the air. *La hojilla* was more recently removed for doing what it had always done – insulting anyone suspected of deviation or softness.

10. Bruce, *The Real Venezuela*, p. 184.

11. *Ibid.*

12. See the various articles by Victor Poleo, an expert on the electricity industry, at www.soberania.net. Poleo was at one stage an adviser to the government; his website, which this is, is extremely hostile to the Chávez project, but his expertise and knowledge of the industry is undeniable.

13. Mike Gonzalez, 'Latin America and the future of the Farc', in *International Socialism Journal*, no. 120, Autumn 2008, see www.isj.org.uk.

Chapter 7

1. For an excellent summary of its content, see Tamara Pearson's 'Planning the Next 6 Years of Venezuela's Bolivarian Revolution' at www.venezuelanalysis.com, 6 July 2013.

2. Guillermo Almeyra, 'El peligro principal en Venezuela', in *Aporrea*, 26 May 2013.

3. The contradictions within the Bolivarian republic, however, have allowed that recognition of indigenous communities to co-exist with the persecution of their leaders, like Sabino, murdered as he led his community against the invasion of their ancestral lands by CarboZulia, the state mining company.

Index